Live in Light

5-MINUTE DEVOTIONS FOR TEEN GIRLS

Melanie Redd

ALTHEA
PRESS

For general information on our other products and services or to obtain technical support, please contact our Customer Care Department within the U.S. at (866) 744-2665, or outside the U.S. at (510) 253-0500.

Althea Press publishes its books in a variety of electronic and print formats. Some content that appears in print may not be available in electronic books, and vice versa.

Interior and Cover Designer: Suzanne LaGasa
Photo Art Director: Sue Bischofberger
Editor: Bridget Fitzgerald
Production Editor: Andrew Yackira
Illustration © 2019 Myriam Van Neste
ISBN: Print 978-1-64152-337-0 | eBook 978-1-64152-338-7

This devotional is dedicated to
my amazing daughter, Emily, who is
passionately following her dreams.
I'm so blessed by her and proud of the
woman she is becoming.

Let your light shine before
others, that they may
see your good deeds
and glorify your Father
in heaven.
—Matthew 5:16

INTRODUCTION

When I was in seventh grade, an older girl in my youth group —a junior in high school—approached me and offered to mentor me once a week. Each Wednesday night before church, we'd huddle on the stairs outside the dining hall and talk about life—about guys, about dating, about the Bible, about prayer, and about how to walk more closely with God.

That was just the start of my mentoring life. I've been blessed to receive guidance from many different women—and I've provided guidance, too.

In fact, for over 25 years, I've had the opportunity to teach and speak to girls, teens, and women in both schools and churches. It's been my joy to personally mentor many young women and high school girls in small group settings and one-on-one.

And I've learned a great deal about teen girls from my young adult daughter and her friends. She has taught me so much about the struggles, challenges, joys, heartbreaks, and opportunities for girls. Her insights have been profoundly helpful in writing this book for you.

With this devotional, I hope to give back. It's my prayer that I can serve as a mentor to you. It's my desire to offer you encouragement—through my stories, life experiences, and time spent with God's word—for your own Christian walk.

You're living in one of the most amazing and challenging times in history to be a teen. You're offered more opportunities than any generation before you—in fact, one of my daughter's college business professors said that he's never seen a better climate for women to thrive and succeed.

However, you are also growing up in one of the most challenging times in history. At school, online, in your neighborhood, and possibly at church, you will face temptation. It's all around you.

Staying close to Jesus can be a challenge with so many distractions bombarding you.

That's why I've written this devotional: to offer you affirmation throughout the adventures, challenges, and distractions of life.

Each day, you can open this little book and find a word of hope to take with you on your journey. Often, it is our life experiences that help us understand what the Bible is telling us.

My prayer is that these short devotions will become a strong foundation for your life. I'm asking God to help you live out the Bible verses and apply them to your life, through prayer, reflection, and action.

May he set your feet on a rock and give you a firm place to stand. (Psalm 40:2)

I look forward to taking this adventure with you!

—Melanie

HOW'S YOUR BALANCE?

"There is a time for everything, and a season for every activity under the heavens."
Ecclesiastes 3:1

Like most people your age, you probably have a packed schedule. Cheerleading. Soccer practice. Church events. Time with your family. Homework. A part-time job. Band practice. Projects. Time with friends. Club meetings. Watching your little sisters or brothers. Errands. More homework.

The Bible tells us that there is time for everything. There's a season for every single activity under heaven. But in our daily lives, it doesn't always feel like we have enough time. It's easy to get stressed out when life feels overwhelming.

The pressure can begin to close in and make you feel like you can't breathe. When you start to feel totally swamped, here are a few things that might ease your stress:

Take a few deep breaths. *Inhale deeply and exhale slowly.*

Talk to God about how you're feeling. *Tell him about your anxiety.*

Write out your to-do list. *Then go back over it and put all the tasks in order from most to least important.*

Start with the first task. *One of my favorite authors is Elisabeth Elliot. When stressed, her best suggestion was always to focus only on completing the first task. Once that's done, move on to the next task.*

REFLECT

Over the next week, try out the four suggestions above. See which one works best for you.

GOD KNOWS YOUR LOCATION

"So then, each of us will give an account of ourselves to God."
Romans 14:12

My father has always been one of those dads who worries about me, especially when I travel. When I went to San Antonio, Texas, in college, he wanted to know what time I was leaving. Then he called all along the way to find out where I was at that moment and when I expected to arrive.

Even though I'm a mom with kids now, he still likes to keep track. Recently, my family and I took a road trip, and Dad texted me regularly to find out where we were and when we would get to our destination.

Our heavenly Father is a lot like my dad, keeping close track of all his children. There's never a moment when he's out of range.

He knows about your travels, your choices, and the decisions you make. He's intimately aware, alert, and in touch with the details of your life.

I'm not sure what this will look like, but there will be a day in heaven when each one of us will stand before our great God. The Bible tells us that, on that day, you will give account to God of your life—owning up to all of your actions, the choices you made, and the attitudes you expressed during your life.

REFLECT

God is watching over you and keeping track of the details of your life. How does this make you feel? Will you do anything differently today knowing this truth?

HANDLE AUTHORITY LIKE A PRO

"Have confidence in your leaders and submit to their authority, because they keep watch over you as those who must give an account. Do this so that their work will be a joy, not a burden, for that would be of no benefit to you."
Hebrews 13:17

My first real job (besides babysitting) was working in a fast-food restaurant taking orders, serving customers, and cleaning up. It wasn't glamorous, but it was so much fun to work with other people and get a regular paycheck.

A few weeks into the job, I began to realize that my boss was a difficult person to please. At times, he was even rude and condescending. Not a great guy to work for—but I learned some valuable lessons about authority. I learned to honor the *position* of authority even when the *person* in authority was tough to respect.

Once I concentrated on the work instead of my own feelings, I also learned that if I did a good job, my boss was easier to deal with. My hard work benefitted him *and* me. The harder I worked, the better we both looked. It was a win-win situation, and so what was a tough relationship became much easier to deal with.

Maybe you can relate. Have you ever had a difficult boss, or a teacher or coach who was especially demanding?

REFLECT

Think of any difficult authorities in your life. How can you respect the position even if you don't respect the person?

CALL ON GOD

"Call to me and I will answer you and tell you great and unsearchable things you do not know."
Jeremiah 33:3

How many phone numbers can you recite from memory? If you wanted to call a friend from someone else's phone, would you know the number offhand, or would you have to look it up?

I've got good news for you: When you call on God, you don't have to memorize a phone number. The Creator of this universe invites you to call him—anytime, for any reason. And he promises to answer when you call. No voicemail. No waiting. Just call on him, and he will answer.

And not only that—he will tell you great and unsearchable things. Our Father says that he will tell you secrets you've never heard before. I wonder what secrets he's waiting to reveal to you today? He's only a prayer away. In prayer, you may find the answer to a question, a truth about yourself or others, or a safe place to speak your mind. And you'll experience great peace and hope.

REFLECT

Call out to the Lord today—no phone needed. Whether in a whisper or a shout, talk to him about your life. Ask him to show you those great and unsearchable things you're eager to hear.

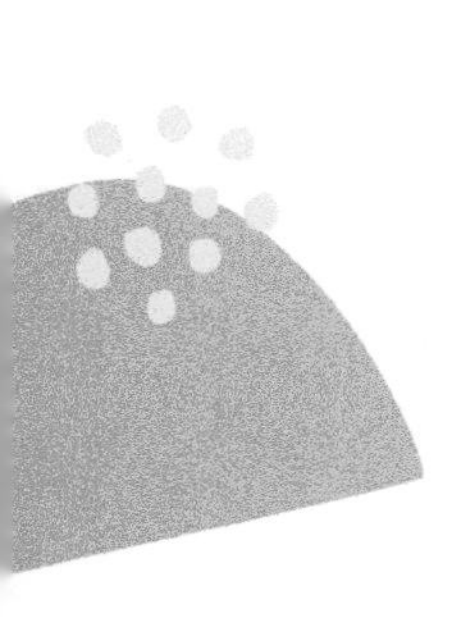

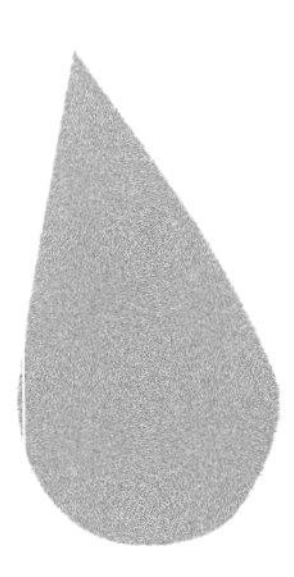

THE PAIN OF REJECTION

"He was despised and rejected by mankind, a man of suffering, and familiar with pain. Like one from whom people hide their faces he was despised, and we held him in low esteem."
Isaiah 53:3

When I was 14, one of my friends and I got into a fight. She soon involved our other friends, and at lunch, they refused to let me sit with them.

This went on for several weeks until our teacher finally sat us all down to talk it out. Things got a little better, but they were never really the same after that.

Being left out is hard for anyone. No one likes to be uninvited, rejected, abandoned, or pushed away. There is something in all of us that loves inclusion and being part of a group.

Jesus personally knew what it was like to be left out. The Bible tells us that he was familiar with the pain of being brushed off. He was greatly despised and mistreated while he walked on this earth. Even some of his closest friends and family members rejected him. When he was arrested, most of his followers and friends deserted him, acting like they didn't even know him.

How did he respond? He showed love. In fact, he gave his life for the very people who rejected him.

We learn to be generous from his example; to shake off the slights of exclusion and bring our best selves forward.

REFLECT

How will you respond when you feel left out or rejected? Think about what you can learn from Jesus's example.

YOU ARE WONDERFULLY MADE

"For you created my inmost being; you knit me together in my mother's womb. I praise you because I am fearfully and wonderfully made; your works are wonderful, I know that full well."

Psalm 139:13-14

When you think of the most beautiful person in the world, who comes to mind? A celebrity? Maybe it's someone you know personally, like a classmate or a friend.

Our culture puts a lot of pressure on young women to be conventionally beautiful, just like the famous faces on TV and online. It's all too easy to start comparing yourself to them and feeling bad about every part of your body—your hairstyle, skin, weight . . . it never seems to end.

However, these images are often deceiving. They've been edited and filtered to look absolutely perfect. Don't compare yourself to these perfected images. They will just make you feel discouraged and unworthy.

There's someone who already thinks you're beautiful, just as you are: our heavenly Father. God made you beautiful. You are a one-of-a-kind original—a masterpiece crafted by him. No one else will ever be exactly like you. You are the only person who's ever lived who has your personality, unique gifts, and DNA. Inside and out, you are gorgeous to God.

REFLECT

Every time you look in the mirror today, look yourself in the eyes and say, "Lord, I praise you because I am beautifully and wonderfully made. Your works are wonderful, God. In my soul—in my deepest parts—I believe this." You can say this out loud or whisper it as a prayer.

SET BOUNDARIES

"Do not move your neighbor's boundary stone set up by your predecessors in the inheritance you receive in the land the LORD your God is giving you to possess."
Deuteronomy 19:14

We once had neighbors who never mowed their lawn—the grass was knee-high and showed no signs of stopping. One day I noticed a stake in the yard with a little pink flag. It indicated a boundary line—a property marker that showed where our yard ended and theirs began. It was a helpful reminder that the overgrown grass was in their yard and it wasn't our problem.

Just as we need boundaries to clearly mark property lines, we also need boundaries in our relationships with our family members and friends. It's healthy to set boundaries around how you spend your time, who you hang out with (or don't), and how you speak and allow others to speak to you.

When people begin to test our boundaries or disrespect them altogether, it can cause problems. Or we might create problems when we brush off other people's boundaries.

The Bible speaks clearly about the need for wise boundaries. As we set up clear markers in our lives, we experience better relationships.

REFLECT

Think about the relationships in your life that need caring for—do any of them involve boundary issues? Are you pushing on anyone else's boundaries without realizing it? Step back and think about how you can fix the situation.

DO GOOD TO OTHERS

"Do not withhold good from those to whom it is due, when it is in your power to act."
Proverbs 3:27

Audrey was only six years old and she had been diagnosed with cancer. All of the tests revealed that she would need to have surgery and then be carefully monitored.

Some friends asked us to reach out to Audrey and her family when they came to St. Jude Children's Research Hospital in our city. We visited with gifts, and this family soon became part of our lives.

Each time they came for tests, checkups, or procedures, we were their designated tour guides. We picked them up and tried to bring some fun into a scary time. Dinners. Bowling. Lots of chocolate desserts. Swimming. Dancing in an empty ballroom. Sightseeing. Shopping. Millions of photos. So much laughter.

It's been more than seven years now. And it's been our joy to watch Audrey grow and win over her cancer. She's doing well and living cancer-free. Our family and her family are deeply connected.

It's biblical. The Bible tells us to do good when we can. You and I need to be kind, generous, and good to others when we have the opportunity.

REFLECT

Who needs something good from you today? Is there someone ill or less fortunate whom you could help? Look for one kind thing you can personally do for someone else today.

CHECK YOUR ANGER

"In your anger do not sin: Do not let the sun go down while you are still angry, and do not give the devil a foothold."
Ephesians 4:26-27

Anger is not a sin. It's the way we handle our anger that can become sinful. When we're angry, we sometimes react by lying, or hurting or disrespecting others. We might even have trouble sleeping. Worst of all? Anger can create a place in our hearts for the devil to set up shop.

It's like my six-month-old Australian shepherd puppy. When he wants to get out of a gate, he inserts one of his floppy white paws into the opening. With a little wiggle room, he can maneuver his entire body out of the gate.

That's how the devil works. He sticks one foot into your anger and tries to tempt you to more anger. Eventually, he will insert himself into a situation completely. This can happen quickly or over several weeks.

Not too long ago, I got really upset with someone. Rather than expressing my hurt, I stuffed it deep inside. Quietly simmering, my anger began to boil over, causing headaches, lack of sleep, and loss of peace. It wasn't until I confessed my feelings to God and let it go that I found relief.

It may be that you are struggling with hurt feelings and anger that you just can't let go of. You might consider talking through these issues with a trusted friend, parent, or counselor.

REFLECT

If you're feeling angry today, don't let the devil stick his foot in and get you really heated. Instead, ask God to calm you down and help you stay that way.

GOD ANSWERS EVERY PRAYER (SERIOUSLY)

"And she said to him, 'Pardon me, my LORD. As surely as you live, I am the woman who stood here beside you praying to the LORD. I prayed for this child, and the LORD has granted me what I asked of him.'"

1 Samuel 1:26-27

Have you ever prayed about something and had God answer in a specific way?

A few years ago our Bible group felt compelled to collect money and give it to a family in our community. We knew they were going through a hard time, so we passed around an offering basket and collected a total of $357.00.

When we gave this gift to the family, they began to cry. They had just received a large bill—none of us could believe it at first, but the amount of the bill was exactly $357.00. Our gift helped them pay the bill on time, giving them some financial stability and peace of mind.

God does not always answer so specifically, in black and white. And yet, you may find he often gives you exactly what you need.

My daughter, Emily, once had a disagreement with some friends, and they started excluding her from their group. Emily was lonely and hurt, and prayed for the friendships to return to the way they once were. But God had a different idea. The following week, a new student started at Emily's school—who eventually became the good friend Emily needed at that time of her life. It was the most amazing and specific answer to her prayer—though not the one she expected.

REFLECT

Ask God for what you need him to do in your life today, and pray for the wisdom to recognize his answer.

BE COMMITTED

"And may your hearts be fully committed to the LORD our God, to live by his decrees and obey his commands, as at this time."
1 Kings 8:61

I fully gave my heart and life to God as a 12-year-old, and I've never looked back. I got a new study Bible and began reading it. My parents bought me a journal where I started recording prayers, dreams, goals, and ideas. At the same time, I began to attend youth events and serve as a volunteer at my church. All of these things changed my life for the better.

Committed. It's to be devoted, faithful, dutiful, and dedicated.

What are you committed to? Maybe your soccer or volleyball team? Or your church youth group? Or your charity work? Perhaps you spend most of your time focused on your studies, or maybe your family and friends are your priority. You may be absolutely intent on having a good time and living life to the fullest. Or you might be committed to a combination of all these things!

In the midst of your busy life, it can be all too easy to let your focus on spirituality slide. That's why, every so often, it's helpful to stop and consider how committed you are to the Lord. What might happen if you decide to be fully committed to Jesus?

REFLECT

How can you serve God with more commitment? Perhaps you can volunteer to work in the church nursery, offer to tutor a younger student, or sign up to go on a mission trip. Consider every opportunity available to you—there may be more than you think.

DEALING WITH DISAPPOINTMENT

"Because he turned his ear to me, I will call on him as long as I live."
Psalm 116:2

I'll never forget the year our family vacation was cut short by a hurricane. One minute, we were sitting in our beach chairs, enjoying the sun, surf, and incredible ocean breeze. The next moment, we were packing up the car, preparing to escape an incoming hurricane. We'd planned to spend a week at the beach; instead, we only got 48 hours. It was a huge disappointment to load up the car and drive away five days early.

Life is filled with disappointments. Our parents' divorce, a breakup, the loss of a friend, failing a test, or not making the squad: Heartbreaks and failures come in all shapes and sizes.

What do you do when you feel disappointed? When life gets hurtful, I've found two steps I can take to feel better. First, when I'm really sad, I go somewhere I can be alone and talk my pain out with God. He understands, and he bends down close to listen when I pray. Father God will do the same for you.

Then, I search for a Bible verse I can turn to for comfort over and over again. I read it, write it in my journal, or text it to myself. Often, soaking in that one verse really lifts my spirits.

REFLECT

Have you experienced any big disappointments recently? How did you respond? Next time you feel let down, try the steps above. Ask God to draw you closer to him and walk with you through your sadness.

HONOR YOUR PARENTS

"Honor your father and your mother, so that you may live long in the land the LORD your God is giving you."
Exodus 20:12

It's always interesting to see how different your mom and dad may be from your friends' parents. Some parents are outgoing and funny; others are more serious. Some are strict; some are more laid-back.

Everyone's family has a different dynamic. Maybe you live with both of your parents, one of them, or maybe you spend time with each parent separately. You might know them well, or you may not feel close to them at all.

Whether the relationship is wonderful or challenging, the Bible commands us to show honor to our father and mother. It's one of the Ten Commandments, in fact. There's no exception: We have to honor them. To honor is show favor, respect, and regard for another person. It's choosing to place value on someone and treat that person with reverence. You honor your parents when you come home when they expect you, or when you wipe down the counter because you know your mom hates a messy kitchen. You can show respect in ways both large and small.

God's word tells us that we will enjoy a long life if we honor our parents. Willingly choosing to esteem your mom and dad will lead to a more positive relationship with them, and your life will be sweeter for it.

REFLECT

Is it easy to show your parents honor and respect, or do you find it difficult? Choose one small step you can take to honor them today—maybe doing a chore around the house or holding your tongue when you're tempted to say something hurtful.

SURROUNDED BY GOD'S LOVE

"May your unfailing love be with us, LORD, even as we put our hope in you."
Psalm 33:22

When I was in college, a girl I knew was walking home alone from the library late one night. It was dark, and she thought she heard someone behind her. Though she was scared, no one bothered her, and she made it safely back to her dorm.

But the story doesn't end there. A few days later, the campus police arrested a suspicious man. When they questioned him, he admitted to following a girl home from the library. He explained that he left her alone because some big guys were walking with her.

My classmates and I were stunned; she had been completely alone. It seemed impossible to explain—but many of us believed the man saw angels surrounding her as she walked alone on that dark night.

The verse in this devotion reminds us that God and his unfailing love are with us all of the time. Like a warm blanket or a group of protectors, God hems us in on every side with his love.

What does this love feel like? Sometimes it's a quiet peace as you walk into a crowded room or take a test at school. At other times, it's a strong emotion that makes you want to lift your voice in worship. As you lay your head on your pillow at night, God's love comes quietly over you and gives you rest. You and I can put our hope in God because he will be with us, surrounding us with his love.

REFLECT

Have you ever felt surrounded by God's love? If you haven't had this experience, take some quiet time to sit by yourself. Ask God to calm your mind, open your heart, and show you just how much he loves you.

DISCOVER HIS FAVOR

"May the favor of the LORD our God rest on us; establish the work of our hands for us—yes, establish the work of our hands."

Psalm 90:17

What is God's favor? It's a special way that God does for us what we cannot do for ourselves. It's having a door opened that you couldn't open yourself. It's when someone who once stood in your way starts supporting you. We experience God's favor when we achieve a goal: making the team, landing the role in a theater production, or getting the grade we studied so hard for.

The Old Testament gives us an example of a follower of Christ who found favor with God, over and over again. Joseph, one of Jacob's 12 sons, was thrown in jail for a crime he didn't commit. But God's favor was upon him, and he was released from jail after using his gift for interpreting dreams to help the Pharaoh. Years later he was promoted to help rule Egypt, second in command to the Pharaoh. Again, God's favor was upon him.

If Joseph's life sounds like an extreme example, think again. God is willing to pour out the most abundant blessings on your life, too.

In Psalm 90, we see a model of how to ask for favor from the Lord. We can pray and ask him to rest his favor on us, inviting him to establish and bless the work of our hands.

Although the Bible doesn't state that Joseph prayed for God's favor, I believe he must have. God's favor was apparent throughout his life, and can be in yours, as well.

REFLECT

Have you experienced God's favor in your life? If so, how? In what ways do you need his favor today? Maybe you've had a fight with your mom, or you clashed with a teacher who's hard on you. Ask God to give you his favor with the people in your life.

HANDLING ANXIETY

"Do not be anxious about anything, but in every situation, by prayer and petition, with thanksgiving, present your requests to God. And the peace of God, which transcends all understanding, will guard your hearts and your minds in Christ Jesus."
Philippians 4:6-7

Anxiety is a very real deal. It can come as a quiet misgiving—that terrible, sinking feeling that something isn't quite right. Or it can present itself in physical symptoms: You might feel your heart racing, your muscles tensing, and your palms getting sweaty.

Tons of people deal with anxiety. It's very common, even in kids and teens. So what can you do when those anxious feelings start to form in the pit of your stomach?

First, you can talk over every situation with God. Prayer calms anxiety. (There are even scientific studies to back this up!) When you present your requests, concerns, and needs to God, he sends you his peace.

Then, allow yourself to enjoy God's peace, which transcends all understanding. In other words, God's peace may not make sense to us, but we get to enjoy it, anyway.

If you feel like your anxiety is overwhelming, it can be helpful to talk to an adult you trust—a parent, coach, or someone at your church. They might suggest that you try seeing a therapist or counselor to help you deal with your anxiety. This is totally normal—lots of people do it and find it really helpful. If you're really struggling and you need help right away, contact the Crisis Text Line by texting HOME to 741741. There's no shame in doing any of these things—God wants you to be happy and healthy!

REFLECT

Let God's peace protect you and give you a calm heart as you go through your day. This is a bit like meditating—slow your breathing and concentrate on the gifts God is giving you.

EXTENDING THE HAND OF FRIENDSHIP

"Therefore, as God's chosen people, holy and dearly loved, clothe yourselves with compassion, kindness, humility, gentleness, and patience."
Colossians 3:12

When I graduated from college, I returned to work in my hometown. It had been four years since I'd lived there and been involved in my community. A group from church was meeting at a restaurant to have dinner. I decided to go, thinking I'd be welcomed back with excitement.

As I walked through the door, I saw that most of the people were already seated at tables all around the large room. I looked for a familiar face, but none of my old friends glanced my way. It seemed they had moved on with their lives and made other friends.

There was nowhere to sit, and I was nearly in tears. I turned to head for the nearest exit—and then a dark-haired young woman I'd never met waved at me. There was an extra chair at her table, and she invited me to sit with her group. In a millisecond, my mood lifted. The rejection and hurt I'd felt was replaced by the sweetest invitation and inclusion.

That girl, Rhonda, went on to become one of my closest friends (and is to this day). On a night when I was feeling crushed by the weight of being left out, she offered me kindness and extended the hand of hospitality.

REFLECT

Recall a time when you were feeling left out until someone extended kindness and warmth to you. Do you try to be friendly to others? How might you be friendlier to someone today?

MERCY: GIVE SOME, GET SOME

"Be merciful, just as your Father is merciful."
Luke 6:36

Mercy looks a lot like compassion, but it's *more*. To offer mercy to another person is to be good to them even when they might not deserve it. Mercy is what leads you to be kind to someone who hurt you—even to forgive them.

God is the greatest giver of mercy. Because of his great love, he holds back his anger, judgment, and wrath. His compassions are never-ending—day after day, he is faithful to us. That's just who he is.

What does this mean for you and for me? It means that we need to give mercy and compassion to others like God gives them to us. Think of it like a giant cup that you fill with God's mercy every single morning. Then, you take your cup and pour it out on others all day long.

If there's a kid at school who seems lonely or isolated, pour out a little mercy on them. If your coach is in a bad mood, share a little mercy. If your mom had a long day at work, let a little compassion spill forth.

REFLECT

Think of someone you know who might be sad, lonely, or in need. How can you show them mercy today? An act of mercy might be as simple as a friendly greeting, a kind word of appreciation, or simply letting the little things slide.

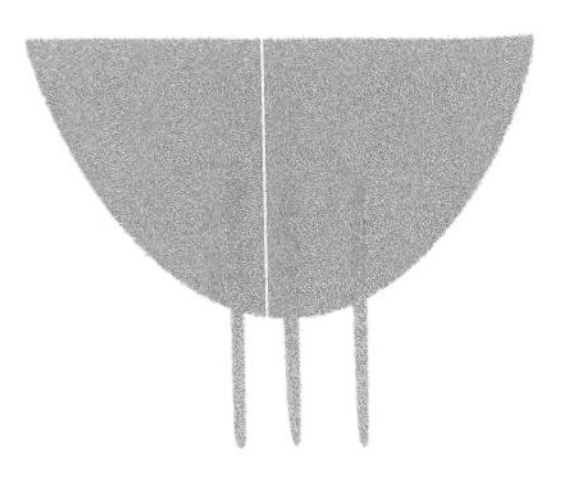

THE STRENGTH TO KEEP GOING

"I have fought the good fight, I have finished the race, I have kept the faith."
2 Timothy 4:7

A few years ago, I ran my first 5k with my daughter and some friends. We got up early on a Saturday morning and joined hundreds of other runners at the starting line. When the buzzer sounded, we were off! Countless people ran alongside us, in front of us, and behind us. As we jogged along, race organizers and friends cheered us on, shouting words of hope. It was grueling, and we got tired at times. But we'd walk a little, catch our breath, and keep going. Eventually, we finished—happy and grateful that we hadn't quit.

Life is a lot like a 5k. You have to get dressed for the race and show up. You begin with excitement and maybe fear, wondering what will happen out there on the course. Sometimes you feel weary and want to stop. At those times, you slow down to a walk, catch your breath, and begin to run again. Every so often, people along the course cheer you on—those are some of the best moments. Most of the time, though, it's up to you to keep going.

To fight the good fight, finish the race, and keep the faith—this is the challenge. Yet our work, efforts, and faithfulness are worthwhile. None of our work for the Lord is in vain. Everything we do for Christ matters.

Can I give you a word of encouragement? Keep going. Nothing that you do for Christ is wasted. What you do for eternity is essential.

REFLECT

Are you weary in the race today? Remember that you can slow down and rest without dropping out of the race.

RESPECT FOR ALL

"Show proper respect to everyone, love the family of believers, fear God, honor the emperor."
1 Peter 2:17

If you could invite anyone to come to your house for dinner this weekend, who would it be? A famous musician, actor, politician, or athlete? Or maybe there's an older student or teacher you'd love to get to know better?

It's easy to imagine sharing a meal with someone famous, popular, or wealthy. But what if I told you that someone else was coming over for dinner on Friday? What if your parents brought a couple of strangers into your home? Or what if your mom decided to invite your most challenging classmate or teammate—perhaps someone you've had disagreements with in the past? That might be tough.

Though it can be difficult to deal with challenging personalities, the Bible encourages us to show respect for everyone. It teaches us to deeply respect God, honor our leaders, and love all people. There's no exception in this verse—no clause that gets you out of the job of respecting even those who are difficult to love and honor.

REFLECT

Think of someone it's not easy for you to respect. Who do you struggle to love? Why is this? How might you show respect for this person?

THERE'S NO SUCH THING AS "PERFECT"

"So God created mankind in his own image, in the image of God he created them; male and female he created them."
Genesis 1:27

Instagram has completely changed the way many teenagers look at themselves. It can be a great way to connect with your friends and share your favorite moments. But the app has a dark side: Whether you realize it or not, it puts a lot of pressure on young women.

On Instagram, you scroll through post after post showing your friends looking fabulous and having the time of their lives. On the surface, there's nothing wrong with that. It's natural to want to show the best version of yourself to the world.

The problems start when you begin to compare yourself to the people you follow, feeling envious or experiencing a drop in your own self-esteem. It's all too easy to try to combat these negative emotions by fixating on the app even more: How many followers do you have? What should you take pictures of? How often should you post?

The reality is that none of the people you follow always look perfect. They're not always out having fun, dressed in the trendiest clothes. They have bad days and good days, just like you.

When you need to remind yourself of this, look to the Bible. In Genesis, we discover that God created us in his image. God created *you* in his own image. And he loves the way he designed you.

When you post something on Instagram, do it to make God smile. Your followers don't matter nearly as much as he does.

REFLECT

Are you overly concerned with comments and follows? When you remember that God created you in his image, does it change how you use social media?

GOD KNOWS YOUR PURPOSE

"The LORD will vindicate me; your love, LORD, endures forever—do not abandon the works of your hands."
Psalm 138:8

When you look ahead at your future, what do you see? Going to college? Falling in love? Marriage? Career? Making a difference in the world?

One of the exciting things about being young is that you have so many significant events to look forward to. There's so much on the horizon! One of the sweet promises of the Bible is that God will accomplish everything that needs to happen in your life. He will help you achieve the goals that are aligned with his will for you. Father God will finish what he started.

If he has been stirring you to write, for example, he will continue to give you words. If your deepest passion is to help or lead others, he can easily open doors for you to do so. Maybe you have a passion for missions, or design, or medicine, or sports. The Lord can teach you, equip you, train you, help you, and move you where you need to be.

Father God is ultimately the one who will get you where you need to be.

REFLECT

What are your biggest hopes and dreams? Pray about them and ask God to give you the courage and strength to pursue them.

CAUTION SIGNS

"Be very careful, then, how you live—not as unwise but as wise, making the most of every opportunity, because the days are evil. Therefore do not be foolish, but understand what the LORD'S will is. Do not get drunk on wine, which leads to debauchery. Instead, be filled with the Spirit."
Ephesians 5:15-18

There are caution signs all around you in life. You'll encounter situations in which you're forced to choose between following the crowd by doing something you don't feel comfortable doing, or sticking to your values and risking rejection. At a sleepover, for example, you may face choices on what movies to watch, what to eat, what to drink, and whether or not to kiss someone. At a party, your caution lights might start flashing when someone spikes the punch or hands you a beer.

Everyone faces temptation, and throughout your life, there will be times when you might be tempted to follow the crowd and do something you feel is wrong: experiment with drugs, make fun of someone on social media, or engage in sexual activity with someone you're dating.

When temptation strikes, it can be helpful to turn to God's word. The Bible tells us directly that we should not act foolishly. Instead, try to focus on God's will for your life. Though others will try to convince you otherwise, you don't need alcohol or drugs to feel good. Only God can give you true peace and happiness.

REFLECT

Are you facing any temptations right now, perhaps from friends pressuring you to act a certain way? If so, talk to an adult you trust.

TRUST IN GOD

"Those who know your name trust in you, for you, LORD, have never forsaken those who seek you."
Psalm 9:10

At a retreat a few years ago, the leader organized us into pairs and announced that we were going to play the trust game. One person had to cover their eyes with a bandana. Their partner's job was to tell them how to walk around the retreat center using only voice commands.

At first, the game was scary. It was unnerving to walk forward without seeing where I was going. But my partner gave me directions for each step. After just a few minutes, it became easier to trust my partner because I believed she was reliable.

Trusting someone means placing your complete confidence in them. When you really trust someone, you confide in them, believing they're a person of character who wants the best for you. Trust indicates reliance and faith. Without a doubt, Scripture teaches us that we can trust in God. He is entirely reliable.

REFLECT

If I asked you to list three people you deeply trust, whom would you name? Your parents, a teacher, your pastor? Or maybe there's someone else you turn to for advice and guidance—a youth minister or friend. How have you experienced their reliability? Thank God for this person (or people!).

SEEK WISDOM

"Do not forsake wisdom, and she will protect you; love her, and she will watch over you. The beginning of wisdom is this: Get wisdom. Though it cost all you have, get understanding."
Proverbs 4:6-7

Losing something important is the worst feeling. We've all lost things we really need—car keys, a cell phone, a textbook. It's annoying, but it's a normal part of life. Once, my entire family spent an hour trying to find the car keys after a party—it was my 18-month-old son who "found" them: in the laundry hamper, where he'd put them.

Sometimes, though, we need to look for things we don't even realize are lost.

Scripture encourages us to search for wisdom—to seek for it with all we have. Wisdom can be defined in many ways, but, at its essence, it means having the courage and strength to live life according to the gospel—loving others and loving God. Wisdom protects us, watches over us, and assists us in life.

Where do you find this wisdom? It's found in the Bible, in prayer, in worship, in relationships with other believers, and in reading great books. Two that I've read and loved are *Whisper* by Mark Batterson and *Unexpected* by Christine Caine. Gaining wisdom is essential to the life of a believer.

REFLECT

Are you on a search for wisdom? Where have you found it lately? Maybe look for some older students or teammates who seem wise. Watch their lives. Model their behavior.

CHURCH IS A VERB

"Every day they continued to meet together in the temple courts. They broke bread in their homes and ate together with glad and sincere hearts, praising God and enjoying the favor of all the people. And the LORD added to their number daily those who were being saved."
Acts 2:46-47

We attend a small church that meets in a multi-purpose room. It's nothing fancy, and the congregation is primarily made up of older adults, with just a few children and young adults. Though it's a small community, it's an active one. We love to sing, study the Bible, host programs like vacation Bible school, and support missions.

In biblical times, church members like those in the verse above met at the temple. Then they'd eat communal meals in each other's homes. They enjoyed God's favor and sweet fellowship with each other. We can see in this verse that God blessed the early church.

Just like that early community, you and I still need the accountability, fellowship, prayer support, and encouragement that community worship offers. Whether you meet in a gym, a coffee shop, someone's home, or a traditional church building, community with other believers is essential.

How would you describe your church? Is it large or small? Traditional or more contemporary? When you think about your community—its members, mission, and style of worship—you can see how it has helped shape the person you are today.

REFLECT

Why does it matter that you go to church? How does your Christian community help you grow in faith?

KINDNESS TO THOSE WHO HURT US

"Be kind and compassionate to one another, forgiving each other, just as in Christ God forgave you."
Ephesians 4:32

I once knew a man who'd done and said some things that hurt me. As a result, being around him was a challenge. Whenever we were in the same room, I'd tense up and get quiet. When people mentioned his name, I'd scowl or say very little about him. In my mind, this man wasn't a nice guy, and I struggled to have a positive relationship with him.

We all know people who make us feel angry or uncomfortable. Just the mention of their name might cause a physical response: You might feel yourself tensing up or becoming awkward.

What should you do when someone hurts you, rejects you, or treats you disrespectfully?

The Bible instructs us to be kind, compassionate, and forgiving. Why? Because this is how God treated us. When we were lost and unlovely, God sent Jesus to die for us. His death offers us new life. In our sin, our heavenly Father offered us incredible grace.

Compassion and forgiveness are not always the easy way to live. However, to really enjoy freedom in Christ and better relationships with others, it's the only way.

REFLECT

Is it hard for you to deal with those who've treated you poorly? Think of someone you need to forgive, and do it today—not tomorrow.

A BEAUTIFUL HEART

"Charm is deceptive, and beauty is fleeting; but a woman who fears the LORD is to be praised."
Proverbs 31:30

One of the scariest days of my life was the morning I woke up with pain in my chest and both of my shoulders. I feared I might be having a heart attack. We rushed to the emergency room, where doctors immediately started running tests.

After the danger had passed, the doctor showed me a monitor. On it was an image of my heart. He told me that it looked lovely. In fact, he said that I had a beautiful heart.

His words stuck with me long after I recovered from the infection that had caused the pain. I loved the idea that I had a beautiful heart muscle—free of any physical ailments. Thinking about my physical heart made me think about something else. If that doctor had been able to x-ray my spiritual heart, what would he have found? In my attitudes, in my choices, and in my way of life, was my spiritual heart also lovely?

The Bible often describes our heart as the core of our being—the center of our minds, emotions, and wills.

So, how's your heart? Not the organ, but the core of your being. Do you have a beautiful heart? The person who worships and honors God is gorgeous. She has a beauty that transcends the limitations of a physical body. There's something that draws people to her. It's her lovely heart.

REFLECT

If we x-rayed your spiritual heart today, what would it look like? Concentrate on having a lovely heart formed by loving thoughts, emotions, and attitudes.

NOT JUST ANOTHER BOOK

"Keep this Book of the Law always on your lips; meditate on it day and night, so that you may be careful to do everything written in it. Then you will be prosperous and successful."
Joshua 1:8

It's one of my favorite of all the books I own: a brown leather Bible given to me by my father. What makes this particular Bible so special? It's filled with sermon notes, quotes, and messages from my childhood pastor. Each time I open the book, I'm reminded of that great man and the impact his life had on mine. He's in heaven now, but his Bible connects me with him.

I once taught a boy who was constantly late to class. One day, he walked in with a soft drink in each hand, kicking a book—a Bible—down the hall ahead of him. In a world of distractions, it's easy to think that the Bible is just another book. But it's so much more than that.

If you study the Bible, you'll notice that the writers often emphasize memorizing, meditating on, and talking about the text. What's more, the Scripture actually promises success and prosperity if you make God's word essential in your life.

For me, the Bible has provided guidance, refuge, and a way of communicating with the God who created me. That's worth more respect than any old book.

REFLECT

How might you make a bigger deal out of the Bible? You may want to attend a small group or a Bible study class. Or pick up a Bible study workbook at a local Christian bookstore. There are also many Bible studies online. Check out SheReadsTruth.com for more info.

KINDNESS IS ITS OWN REWARD

"Whoever is kind to the poor lends to the LORD, and he will reward them for what they have done."
Proverbs 19:17

God's economy operates differently. We give, we share, we lend, and he rewards us for what we do. That reward doesn't always come in the form of material things like money or clothes. Sometimes God rewards us in more meaningful ways.

On a mission trip years ago, our interpreter was a beautiful Romanian woman. She was warm and friendly, with a great sense of style, and she was curious about Jesus. During our trip, she asked us many questions about grace, faith, and God.

On our last day, she shared that she didn't own a Bible. Since we were in a country that had just pushed off the tyranny of communism, there were no stores to buy one. I felt prompted to give her my personal Bible, a gesture that touched her so deeply that she was moved to tears.

I didn't get a tangible reward that day—something I could hold or display. Instead, my reward was to witness her authentic emotion at receiving her own copy of the Truth. Maybe one day I'll find out how giving her my Bible impacted her life.

REFLECT

Is there anyone in your life who could use the gift of your generosity? Think of the intangible gifts you have to give, such as your time, appreciation, or a shoulder to cry on.

PREPARED IN ADVANCE

"For we are God's handiwork, created in Christ Jesus to do good works, which God prepared in advance for us to do."
Ephesians 2:10

When I was in elementary school, we lived in a neighborhood with families who only had boys. I grew up playing sports and riding bikes with a whole gang of them.

One of my favorite things to do was play "school" with the whole crew. I'd set up a classroom in my playroom and have them all sit at desks. The boys were the students, and I was their teacher.

Many years later, I became a real classroom teacher. All of that practice when I was a kid gave me a little boost of confidence as I taught. I was prepared in advance.

That's because God prepares us for our mission in life. You are God's handiwork, created in Christ Jesus to do good works. From the beginning of time, God made a plan for your life. He equipped you with certain gifts, talents, abilities, and inclinations that were woven into your DNA long before the world began. It's pretty amazing to consider!

What do you think God is preparing you to do? Have you taken the time to think about it? What are some of your talents? What comes easily to you? What makes you unique and special?

REFLECT

Take a minute to write down five things that make you special. Ask God to show you today how he wants to use you and your unique gifts.

BUILDING BRIDGES

"If it is possible, as far as it depends on you, live at peace with everyone."
Romans 12:18

Have you ever watched a bridge being built? It's pretty impressive. Huge cement beams are driven deep into the ground to give the structure a firm foundation. Then the beams are fortified with metal scaffolding and concrete to strengthen the supports. Finally, the roadway is built on top of the supports to allow cars to travel.

Building relationships can be a little like building a bridge. You need a foundation—often a shared interest, background, or goal upon which to build your relationship. In Christ, believers find meaningful fellowship with other believers. You also need support beams that will strengthen your relationship, like common dreams and values. And you'll need the actual roadway that allows you to interact, communicate, and relate—perhaps a weekly meeting or an active email chain. But just building a bridge is not always enough.

Ideally, we try to build relationships with everyone. Scripture tells us to live at peace with others as much as we possibly can; however, there will be times when you might not be able to form a friendship with someone. But there's no need to force it. You can seek to build a bridge with someone and meet them in the middle, but you can't demand that anyone pass over it to become your friend. They must choose to accept you and your friendship from their own hearts.

REFLECT

Think about the people who bring you joy—those you're close to, and those you might not know that well. Are there any friendships you'd like to establish? What steps can you take to build a bridge with them?

HOW'S YOUR MIND-SET?

"Finally, brothers and sisters, whatever is true, whatever is noble, whatever is right, whatever is pure, whatever is lovely, whatever is admirable—if anything is excellent or praiseworthy—think about such things."

Philippians 4:8

My friend Valerie is funny, kind, genuine, and a blast to be around. Over the years, we've taken road trips, attended conferences, eaten great food, prayed together, and laughed like crazy. In my opinion, she can do anything. But she once said the most interesting thing. She told me that when she gets ready to try something new, she always doubts she'll be successful. But she saw that I always entered into new pursuits believing I could accomplish anything. We had different mind-sets, and she admired mine.

How's your mind-set? Do you believe you can do whatever you set out to do? Are you full of self-confidence or plagued by insecurity?

I'm blessed to have a natural inclination toward focusing on things that are good, true, and admirable. Things that are excellent and praiseworthy fill my thoughts, and this makes all the difference in how I approach challenges, both old and new.

Valerie, on the other hand, suffered from "stinkin' thinkin'" (as so many people do!).

The Bible encourages us to set our minds on good things, positive things, possible things. Doing this is a choice. We have to regularly focus our attention on what's good and noble, and that's work. If you're willing to put in the work, though, you'll find that you reap huge rewards.

REFLECT

How's your thinking? Are you more like Valerie or like me? If you struggle, what can you do to get your mind and your thoughts on better things?

FEELING CRUSHED

"We are hard pressed on every side, but not crushed; perplexed, but not in despair; persecuted, but not abandoned; struck down, but not destroyed."
2 Corinthians 4:8-9

Every Thursday morning in my neighborhood, an unconventional garbage truck makes its rounds. It's equipped with a grinder that picks up tree branches, boxes, and small household objects and crushes them to bits. You can hear the smashing and grinding as the truck winds its way through the streets.

You've probably discovered that things will happen to you and around you that threaten to crush you. You may feel pressured or smothered by your family and friends. Or maybe you've felt the sting of being persecuted for your faith. The challenges of this world can begin to close in on you.

You may be pressed on every side, afflicted, burdened, and pressured. You may not know where to turn, but you don't have to give in to despair.

There is always hope. You can trust in the fact that God will never leave you alone. He will never abandon you or force you to fight your battles by yourself. When you feel crushed, he offers peace and encouragement. Press in close to Jesus. Talk over your hurts with him. Allow his grace to support you and his love to surround you.

In Christ, we always have hope!

REFLECT

What's the most crushing thing you've ever had to face? How did you get through it? Where do you find your greatest hope and courage?

BROTHERS AND SISTERS

"Bear with each other and forgive one another if any of you has a grievance against someone. Forgive as the LORD forgave you."
Colossians 3:13

My friend Alex grew up with one brother and one sister. Her sister was easy to love and so much fun. But her brother was a challenge. His temper and cutting remarks often reduced Alex to tears.

As she got older, she realized she was holding onto some real bitterness toward her brother. Although he'd never asked for forgiveness, she knew she had to let go of her hurt feelings. Because God had showed Alex abundant grace and forgiveness, it was impossible for her not to show that same grace and forgiveness to her brother.

If you have brothers and sisters, I'm sure you've felt at times that your relationship is far from perfect. We often fight with those we love the most. And when we fight, we say hurtful and insensitive things that we don't really mean.

When that happens, the Bible instructs us to bear with each other and forgive each other. When negative feelings build up inside and cause us anger, God asks us to forgive. Forgiveness is an important tool in families, classrooms, teams, at work—almost every situation in life.

REFLECT

How can you forgive someone who's hurt you? First, pray for the person who caused you pain. Talk to God about them. Second, ask God to drain your anger toward this person. Third, why not try an honest conversation with the person who hurt you? Invite them to coffee and calmly share your heart and your hurt. Try to understand their perspective and what might have caused their behavior. When people are hurt, they often hurt others.

HOW TO MAKE GOD HAPPY

"And without faith it is impossible to please God, because anyone who comes to him must believe that he exists and that he rewards those who earnestly seek him."

Hebrews 11:6

Faith is a big deal to God. Entire chapters in the Bible are devoted to the subject of faith and faithful people. But what *is* faith, exactly? And why does it matter so much?

In simple terms, faith is a deep trust that God is who he says he is and has the power to do what he says he can do. It's trusting what you cannot see and don't understand—even when it may make no sense at all.

Think about it: We exercise faith in the airlines every time we get on a plane. Each time you ride in a car, you exercise faith that your vehicle will start and carry you safely to your destination.

You put your faith in your teachers when you take notes and listen. Faith in your coaches comes when you trust their game plan. To put your faith in your parents is to trust them to provide for you and protect you.

The Bible tells us that it's impossible to make God happy unless we exercise faith. And he rewards us when we believe him, trust in his existence, and seek him with all of our hearts.

REFLECT

What keeps you from exercising greater faith? In what area of your life would you like to have greater faith?

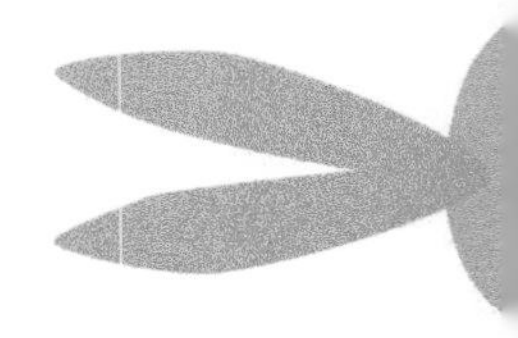

FEAR OF MISSING OUT

"So do not fear, for I am with you; do not be dismayed, for I am your God. I will strengthen you and help you; I will uphold you with my righteous right hand."
Isaiah 41:10

Fear grips all of us at times. As a human race, we have a lot of fears in common: the fear of pain, the fear of loneliness, the worry that we'll miss out.

Then there are fears that fit into the "what if?" category. What if I never learn to drive? What if they don't like me? What if I don't get into college? What if everyone is hanging out without me? The things we're afraid of may never actually happen—but sometimes we just can't help worrying about them.

Do you find yourself anxious and worried about what might (or might not) happen in your life? Do you worry you've made the wrong choice or missed out on something?

The Bible talks a great deal about fear and how to deal with it. In this verse, God is encouraging the people of Israel not to fear. This is the message he's giving you: Because he's with you, he promises to strengthen and help you. He will lead you and uphold your choices. It's possible someone out there witnesses your choices—to spend time with your family, to attend church, to concentrate on your studies—and worries they are missing out on those very same opportunities and experiences.

REFLECT

Don't let the fear of missing out overwhelm you. Why not try this experiment each time you begin to worry about something: Talk about the fear with God, and invite him to fill you with his peace. It can also be helpful to talk to a good friend, or an adult you're close to—perhaps a parent, older cousin, or grandparent. When you confess your fears, you might be surprised at how many other people have been afraid of the very same thing.

THE SECRET TO HAPPINESS

"I am not saying this because I am in need, for I have learned to be content whatever the circumstances. I know what it is to be in need, and I know what it is to have plenty. I have learned the secret of being content in any and every situation, whether well fed or hungry, whether living in plenty or in want."

Philippians 4:11-12

For most of my life, my grandmother lived in a tiny home in a small Mississippi town. She never wore expensive clothes or took exotic vacations. In fact, she never ventured out much at all. However, she was a happy person—generous, kind, and wonderful to be around.

What was her secret? My grandmother had learned to enjoy her life as it was. She had discovered how to be content no matter her circumstances. Her life was beautiful, and it was enough.

In this verse, Paul tells the church at Philippi how to be happy. Maybe that's where my grandmother learned it.

New clothes and shoes, the newest cell phone, a brand-new car, and more money are great, but they won't bring you lasting satisfaction. Why? Because as soon as we get those things, we always find ourselves wanting more.

Contentment comes when you realize that what you have right now is enough.

REFLECT

Do you ever struggle to be content? Do you find yourself wanting more? How might your life change if you found contentment with where you are, what you have, and the people who surround you *right now*?

AVOIDING GOSSIP

"A perverse person stirs up conflict, and a gossip separates close friends."
Proverbs 16:28

When you were a kid, you probably played that game in which players sit in a circle and one person starts the game with a secret sentence. They whisper it to their neighbor, who turns to their neighbor and does the same. Eventually, the secret makes it all the way around the circle.

Typically, the secret sentence has been completely changed by the time it reaches the end of the circle. Some players misheard what their neighbor said to them, causing them to pass on the wrong message to *their* neighbor. Usually, by the end of the game, the sentence doesn't even sound like the message that began the game.

In some places, this game is called "gossip." And it's a good name, because it's exactly what gossip is like. Words whispered in secret pass from one person to another. Each retelling adjusts the message slightly. As the gossip spreads, so do the inaccuracies, misunderstandings, and hurt.

In Proverbs, God discourages us from stirring up conflict and sharing gossip. Maybe you have a friend who's constantly talking about people behind their backs and creating drama. You might be tempted to do the same.

But creating drama and gossiping about others never ends well. It's all too easy to damage a friendship with careless words. Be wise with the stories you share, and even more careful with the stories shared with you.

REFLECT

Have any of your friendships suffered because of gossip? Why is it so tempting to stir up conflict? When someone starts gossiping, you might change the subject, or say, "I don't feel comfortable talking about this person behind their back."

GOD'S TO-DO LIST

"Praise the LORD, my soul, and forget not all his benefits—who forgives all your sins and heals all your diseases, who redeems your life from the pit and crowns you with love and compassion, who satisfies your desires with good things so that your youth is renewed like the eagle's."

Psalm 103:2-5

I'm willing to bet you have a to-do list somewhere. Where do you keep yours? In a planner or on your phone?

Your typical daily list might include things like: wake up, take a shower, eat breakfast, pray, get dressed, go to classes all day, head to sports or drama practice, eat dinner, do homework, talk to friends, walk the dog, get ready for bed, and get some sleep. That's a lot—and it may not even be everything! Maybe you have a job, a boyfriend, and all sorts of church and club activities to add to your list.

God has a to-do list as well. Psalm 103 gives us a pretty good idea of some of the things that God does in a day—like forgiving us our daily sins, healing us when we're sick, satisfying us and giving us joy in our work, and filling us with the strength to do all that we need to do.

He's a good God, and he's good to you and to me.

REFLECT

Look back over God's to-do list from today. What do you most appreciate that he does regularly for you? Take a moment and thank him for his kindness and care.

YOUR SPIRITUAL GIFT

"Each of you should use whatever gift you have received to serve others, as faithful stewards of God's grace in its various forms."

1 Peter 4:10

One of the best gifts I ever received was a complete surprise. My friend Lynn knew how much I wanted to see the play *Wicked*. However, finances were tight, and I didn't feel right splurging on tickets. On my birthday, she handed me a beautiful gift bag. Inside were two tickets to see the musical. And they were in the third row. What an incredible gift!

God loves to give gifts, too. And he's given you a very special one. According to the Bible, it's a spiritual gift: a supernatural way that the Holy Spirit works through your life to help others, glorify God, and bring about his kingdom on earth.

My main spiritual gift is exhortation. God uses me to creatively encourage other people through what I write, blog, and speak. Often, the Lord will bring someone to mind, and I'll send that person a text or email to encourage them and let them know I'm praying for them. These are just some of the ways I use my gift.

There is nothing sweeter than allowing God to use our spiritual gifts to impact other people.

REFLECT

So, what's your gift? How does God use you to bless others and glorify himself? If you aren't sure, take a spiritual gift assessment online (just Google "free spiritual gift test").

FILLED TO OVERFLOWING

"May the God of hope fill you with all joy and peace as you trust in him, so that you may overflow with hope by the power of the Holy Spirit."
Romans 15:13

When my daughter was in high school, I always knew when she was short on cash. She and her friends would pool their money to fill the family car's tank with just $5 or $10 of gas—just enough to last until their next paycheck. You've probably been there.

Have you noticed that a lot of Christian teens live on small amounts of spiritual cash? They grab a little inspiration on Sunday at church, then listen to a little Christian music in the car, and maybe drop by youth group during the week to get a little encouragement. However, their spiritual tanks of hope stay pretty close to empty most of the time.

But God didn't set it up for us to live this way. In the Bible, he promises that we can be filled with all joy and peace. We can overflow with hope by the power of the Holy Spirit. Your tank doesn't have to be dry; make a full tank the norm.

So how do you get more hope in your life? The Scriptures tell us to trust in him. Draw up close to God, pray, read the Bible, spend time with others who love the Lord, and focus your attention on him. That's how your spiritual tank gets filled.

REFLECT

How full is your tank? If it's feeling low, what's one thing you can do this week to fill it up?

LEARNING FROM OTHERS

"Whatever you have learned or received or heard from me, or seen in me—put it into practice. And the God of peace will be with you."
Philippians 4:9

At one time or another, you've probably had a favorite teacher—someone who actually made learning fun, or was compassionate toward everyone in the class. Teachers have a powerful impact on our lives, as do coaches, youth ministers, pastors, and other mentors.

Mentors are people who have walked a little further ahead of us on the spiritual path; they call back to us with wise instruction and insights. They can help us take better paths and avoid wasteful detours. Having a mentor—or several—can save you a lot of time and trouble.

The Apostle Paul was a mentor to the church at Philippi. In fact, Paul encouraged the Philippian people to learn from him. Telling people to follow his example might sound like an arrogant thing to do. But Paul wasn't arrogant—he was giving himself to these believers, whom he loved dearly, as a positive mentor.

Who are your mentors at this juncture in your life? Who are those older, wiser people who give you great counsel and advice? Maybe your mentor is a coach or teacher, an older teammate, or a woman at church whom you respect?

If you don't have any mentors, that's okay, too. Start searching for one, and ask God to lead you to the right person.

REFLECT

Name some mentors you have right now. How do you benefit from time together? If you don't have a mentor, talk to your parents, youth minister, or another adult about how to find one.

FEELING LONELY

"Do not fear, for I have redeemed you; I have summoned you by name; you are mine. When you pass through the waters, I will be with you; and when you pass through the rivers, they will not sweep over you. When you walk through the fire, you will not be burned; the flames will not set you ablaze."

Isaiah 43:1-2

It's normal to feel lonely sometimes. Loneliness penetrates the hearts of all of God's children and causes us to feel invisible, unwanted, unnoticed, and unhappy. Loneliness has many causes: hurt feelings, missed invitations, or simply a weary mind that needs rest.

What can you do when the waves of loneliness crash over your heart? The Bible encourages us to remember a few things when life gets hard. First, remember that the God who created you calls you by name. He knows where you live, what you're dealing with, and how much it hurts. Second, remember that you are never alone—no matter how hard things seem right now, God always walks beside you.

When you're struggling with loneliness, it's helpful to let someone know. Call, text, or talk to a trusted friend, parent, teacher, coach, or youth pastor, and let them know that you are struggling. Uncovering the truth can bring healing to your heart.

Another tactic is to give other people what you need. It may sound counterintuitive, but it really helps. So go to that Bible study, invite a friend to coffee, and put yourself out there—even if you don't feel like it. You might be surprised to find that when you reach out to others, some of your loneliness dissipates.

REFLECT

Whatever you do, remember that you don't have to stay in a lonely place. Trust that God never leaves you alone.

GOD LOVES MUSIC, TOO

"Praise the LORD. Praise God in his sanctuary; praise him in his mighty heavens. Praise him for his acts of power; praise him for his surpassing greatness. Praise him with the sounding of the trumpet, praise him with the harp and lyre, praise him with timbrel and dancing, praise him with the strings and pipe, praise him with the clash of cymbals, praise him with resounding cymbals."

Psalm 150:1-5

If you were to check out my playlist, you'd find everything from Michael Jackson to Lauren Daigle to Carrie Underwood. What's your favorite kind of music? Do you like pop, rock, country, rap, or a little bit of everything? What's your favorite band or singer? What groups are at the top of your playlist?

Music is a universal language, spoken across the world. Anyone can listen to and appreciate it, no matter their age, culture, wealth, or education level.

God gave us the gift of music, and he loves it, too. If he has a mobile device and a playlist, I'd love to find out what's on it. He's likely listening to the city church choir as they practice, or the school choir as they rehearse after classes. Maybe he's listening to the young mom who sings lullabies to her newborn baby. Or he might be tuned into the teen girls singing along with the radio at the top of their lungs.

REFLECT

The Psalms encourage us to praise God with our voices, instruments, and dancing. What's your favorite way to praise him? If you play an instrument, sing, or dance, think of how you might lend your talents to praise.

FIND REST

"Come to me, all you who are weary and burdened, and I will give you rest. Take my yoke upon you and learn from me, for I am gentle and humble in heart, and you will find rest for your souls. For my yoke is easy and my burden is light."

Matthew 11:28-30

Do you remember rest time in preschool or kindergarten? It was usually after lunch. The teacher would tell you to grab your mat and stretch out on the floor. Maybe there was a little resting, but mostly it was quiet time spent looking at the ceiling and trying not to giggle.

In Matthew, the words of Jesus encourage us to rest. When we're weary, we can come to Christ to find rest for our souls.

How do we do this on a practical level? What does it look like? In simple terms, to rest is to grab your mat and spend some quiet time with the Lord. Each day, take a few moments to hang out with the Creator of the universe. Praying, journaling, reading the Bible or a devotion, and listening to praise music are all ways to sit and relax with him.

When you spend quiet time with God, he fills your cup, floods your heart with peace, and gives you strength to face the rest of the day. Time with Jesus teaches you to live more freely and with less stress.

REFLECT

Do you have quiet time with God each day? What does it look like? If you don't yet, when might be the best time to fit this into your day?

GOD HEARS YOUR PRAYERS

"This is the confidence we have in approaching God: that if we ask anything according to his will, he hears us."
1 John 5:14

I visit my mentor, Barbara, a couple of times a month. We'll sit down together to have coffee and talk about life. We talk about our families, our ministries, and about what God is teaching us. Then, we take a few moments and pray for each other.

One of the things I most appreciate about Barbara is the way she listens to me as I talk. She not only nods while I talk, but she also asks follow-up questions and shows a genuine interest in my responses. The way she focuses on my words makes me feel important.

In the same way, you and I have a Father God who's a fabulous listener. You can talk to him, cry to him, whisper to him, call out to him, sing to him, and spill your guts to him. Your God is always available to hear from you.

The Scripture tells us that we can confidently approach his throne, knowing that anything we share, he hears. He's not on his cell phone. He's not busy managing the world. He's not preoccupied with other people. In every moment of every day, the Lord has time for you.

REFLECT

God is listening closely to you, right now. What's in your heart that you'd like to share with him?

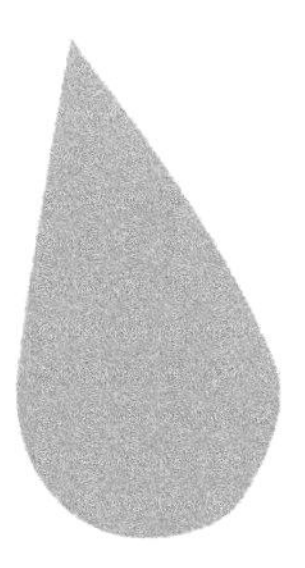

DON'T CRITICIZE

"Why do you look at the speck of sawdust in your brother's eye and pay no attention to the plank in your own eye? How can you say to your brother, 'Let me take the speck out of your eye,' when all the time there is a plank in your own eye?"

Matthew 7:3-4

Lately, I've noticed an increase in the number of people whom I call the "ultra critics." You know who I'm talking about. They're the people who always correct your spelling, criticize your Instagram posts, and generally have an "opinion" about everything. Most people who do this don't even realize they're doing it. Criticizing, making cutting remarks, and autocorrecting everyone just comes naturally to them.

At times, it may feel like there are critics all around you, and their attitude might begin to rub off on you. But the Bible encourages us to behave in exactly the opposite way. Matthew warns us not to fall into the trap of focusing on the speck of sawdust in our friend's eye while remaining ignorant of the plank in our own. In other words: Have humility about your mistakes. You may want to criticize a friend or family member for their mistake, but the reality is that you've probably made plenty of mistakes in your own life, too. Realizing this gives you some perspective and may help you think twice before calling someone out.

Joining the critics is the easy way out—and tempting. It's much more difficult to be the one who lifts someone up when everyone else is tearing them down. Though it's challenging, it's worth it.

REFLECT

I love this anonymous quote I saw on Instagram: "Anyone can find the dirt in another person. Be the one who finds the gold."

YOUR LIFE MOTTO

"The LORD is with me; I will not be afraid. What can mere mortals do to me? The LORD is with me; he is my helper. I look in triumph on my enemies."
Psalm 118:6-7

If you've been part of any sort of organized group or team, you probably had a motto. The Girl Scouts, for example, have always used the motto "Be prepared."

For a community of people working toward a shared goal, having a motto can help them identify themselves and declare their values. Finding a motto for your life can have the same benefits, so I encourage you to find one. Each time you leave your house and enter the world, you can say your motto over and over to yourself. It will become your personal anthem.

For me, the words to this verse have become my life motto. The message is simple: "The Lord is with me. The Lord is for me. I will not be afraid." When I'm preparing to speak to a group of women, I'll go over my motto. The words, "The Lord is for me. The Lord is for me," ring through my head.

You can use my motto or find one of your own. It can be a Scripture verse, a song, or a favorite quote. (Personally, I believe there is great power in Scripture, which is why I chose a verse for my own motto.) Then, write it down. Text it to yourself. Memorize it and start using it on a regular basis.

REFLECT

What Scripture verse, song lyric, or favorite quote might be a great life motto for you?

RUN FOR (ETERNAL) LIFE

"Do you not know that in a race all the runners run, but only one gets the prize? Run in such a way as to get the prize. Everyone who competes in the games goes into strict training. They do it to get a crown that will not last, but we do it to get a crown that will last forever. Therefore I do not run like someone running aimlessly."

1 Corinthians 9:24-26

Do you love the Olympics like I do? There's something so beautiful about sports like figure skating, gymnastics, and diving. It's amazing to watch our athletes compete in the games, knowing how much training and sacrifice goes into every single competition.

But can you imagine an Olympian going to all that trouble and not trying to win a prize? It would be absurd to watch an athlete get to the starting line and then run aimlessly down the track. We want to see the runners bolt off the starting block, running with focus and determination toward the finish line, striving to win the gold medal.

Similarly, the Apostle Paul reminds us to run toward our prize: eternal life with Jesus. Run with purpose, not aimlessly. Run not for an earthly gold medal, but for a crown that will last forever.

In this life, it's easy to lose focus and run aimlessly. Pressure from friends, social media, and family members can distract you in your race. Fix your eyes on Jesus and keep running.

REFLECT

How are you running today? You've started the race; are you squarely headed for the finish line? Ask God to give you strength to keep running.

SPEAK WITH GRACE

"Let your conversation be always full of grace, seasoned with salt, so that you may know how to answer everyone."
Colossians 4:6

Salt is one of my very favorite seasonings. I love it on popcorn, corn on the cob, french fries—almost every food. It's a magical compound that makes everything taste better.

The Bible tells us to be loving and full of grace as we talk to others. When our conversations are seasoned with grace and love—the "salt" in this verse—they "taste" better to others. "Salt" makes people want to listen. We also need to be wise, honest, and seek the right response for every situation.

One of the ways to speak with more grace is to ask God to give you the words. Time spent in prayer can help you become confident when talking to anyone—from your best friend to total strangers. Why not ask God to make you an incredible conversationalist?

To know how to answer everyone—this is a wonderful goal.

REFLECT

How is your speech? Are you gracious with other people? Do you season your words?

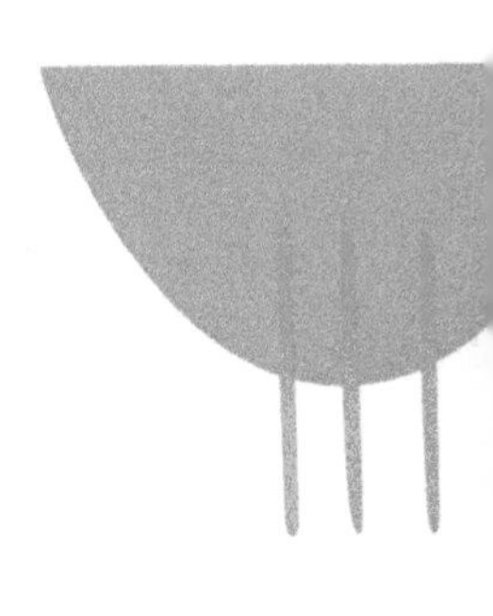

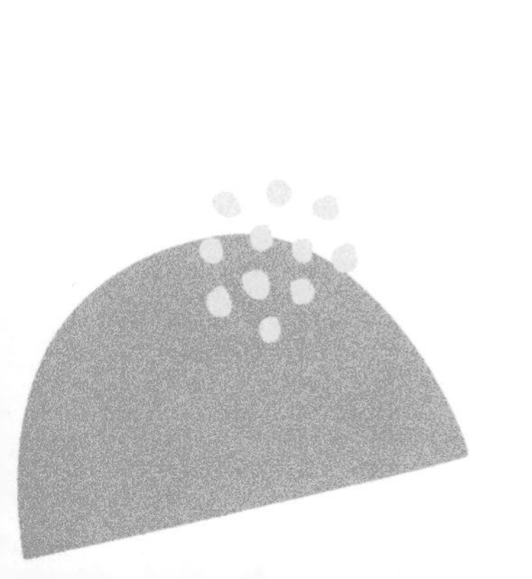

A TROUBLED WORLD

"I have told you these things, so that in me you may have peace. In this world you will have trouble. But take heart! I have overcome the world."
John 16:33

Wars. Famine. Financial crises. School shootings. Car accidents. Divorces. All of these events are heartbreaking and difficult to understand. At times, it can seem like life is filled with tragedy and great pain.

Jesus promised that we would have trouble in this world. Because of the effects of sin and the fall, trouble is part of our lives. And yet, we don't have to be overcome by the tragedies around us. Our Savior said he came to earth to give us peace. Through him, we can overcome anything that happens in this world.

But it can be disheartening, can't it? I once had neighbors who seemed worried and nervous. They were retired, and I knew they watched the news nonstop. I couldn't help wondering if that was the reason why they rarely smiled. The troubles of the world threatened to overwhelm them.

To take heart and overcome feelings of sadness or despair, try to limit how much bad news you watch and listen to. Don't let tragedy consume your thoughts. Instead, take your troubles and lay them before the Savior. Invite him to flood you with his peace.

REFLECT

Do you ever find yourself getting overwhelmed by the tragedies around you? How have you found the peace of Christ to help? When you feel overcome, it may help to talk to a trusted friend or adult. It's normal to feel sad, but you shouldn't live in sadness or fear.

KNOW THE TRUTH

"Then you will know the truth, and the truth will set you free."
John 8:32

Recently, I was talking to a good friend who regularly shares what she's reading and learning with me. She told me about a life-changing new practice she had put into place called "Telling Myself the Truth."

Her life-altering system works like this: Typed on a piece of paper and hanging on her wall are five truths that she reads aloud every single morning. Each truth is based on the truth of God's word—the Bible. As she reads them every day, these truths are becoming realities in my friend's life. Knowing the truth is setting her completely free.

She challenged me to try it, so I typed up my own list of truths to place on my closet wall. I wrote:

The Lord is FOR me. (Psalm 118:6)

God loves me unconditionally. (Romans 8:38–39)

God's grace is enough for anything I will face today. (2 Corinthians 12:9)

God has amazing plans for my future. (Jeremiah 29:11)

Father God will never leave me or forsake me. (Hebrews 13:5)

What about you? If I were to ask you to type up a list of truths that you want to make a reality in your life, what would you add? What are your favorite Bible promises? What words of truth encourage you the most?

REFLECT

Take five minutes and jot down five Bible truths right now. Carry them with you, hang them on your bathroom mirror, or tape them up in your closet. When you know the truth, the truth will set you free.

YOUR GRANDPARENTS

"I am reminded of your sincere faith, which first lived in your grandmother Lois and in your mother Eunice and, I am persuaded, now lives in you also."
2 Timothy 1:5

As Paul begins his second letter to his younger brother in the faith, Timothy, he mentions Timothy's godly mother and grandmother. Timothy's grandmother, Lois, had a profound impact on his life. From this verse, it's clear that she assisted in raising him and instructing him in the faith.

There's something amazing about grandparents. When I was born, every one of my grandparents and great-grandparents was living. As a child, I was lucky to get to spend time with all of them, and they had a powerful impact on my life.

What are your grandparents like? How have they had an impact on your life? What do you most appreciate about them? Whether they're healthy or frail, still living or in heaven, you might be surprised at how much they've influenced you. If you have difficulty remembering them, that's okay, too—ask your mom or dad to tell you about them.

Grandparents are a gift for so many reasons. They step in when our parents are unavailable or busy. They can teach us so many things. They've lived through a lot and learned from so many experiences. They support you and cheer you on. The older you get, the more you realize what a blessing it is to have several generations of people in your corner.

REFLECT

Think about how your grandparents influenced you, and praise God for their wisdom and love.

EVERYTHING CHANGES, EXCEPT GOD

"Jesus Christ is the same yesterday and today and forever."
Hebrews 13:8

Have you noticed how often things change? For example, you get a new cell phone, and a newer model comes out. Or you put on an outfit that's perfect for today's weather, and the temperature changes. Maybe you get comfortable in your school, only to find out your parents' jobs are changing and you have to move.

Change is inevitable. It's part of life. And most of us don't like change or handle it very well. You've likely experienced some sort of change already this week—in your family, at school, in your body, with your friends, or at church. Change happens all the time, no matter how much we try to stop or prevent it.

I've found great hope in knowing that our God never changes. The Bible tells us he is the same yesterday, today, and forever. Think about this for a moment. The God that you worship is the same God that your grandparents and great-grandparents worshipped.

God was faithfully the same for Christians such as George Washington Carver, Florence Nightingale, C. S. Lewis, Rosa Parks, and Martin Luther King, Jr. Throughout the pages of the New Testament, God never changed for people like the Apostle Paul, Mary, Martha, Timothy, and Peter. And, in the Old Testament, he was faithful in the lives of everyone from Adam and Eve to Malachi.

God never, ever changes. He is always faithful and constantly dependable.

REFLECT

Think about all the Christians throughout history who have worshipped the same faithful God. How has God been faithful in your life?

LET'S TALK ABOUT DATING

"Do not be misled: 'Bad company corrupts good character.'"
1 Corinthians 15:33

What do you look for in a guy? Good looks, a sense of humor, a warm personality, or maybe big blue eyes? Attraction is fickle and sometimes very hard to describe. When you ask your friends why they like a certain guy, I'm willing to bet that a lot of them say, "He's cute," or, "He's so sweet."

The Bible warns us to be careful about the people we spend time with. To keep from being misled, it helps to make a list of traits you're looking for in a boyfriend (or any friend, for that matter).

Here are a few that I shared with my daughter when she first started dating. This isn't a complete list, but it may give you some things to think about:

- Is he a gentleman?
- Does he treat you kindly and with respect?
- Is he a good friend to his friends?
- Does he get along with his teachers, coaches, and parents?
- Does he love Jesus?
- Do you trust him?
- Does he have a good sense of humor?
- Do you enjoy being around him?
- Does he make you feel good about yourself?

REFLECT

Make a list of at least 10 great qualities you're looking for in a guy you'd hope to date. Be specific and set high standards now. You'll never be sorry you did!

BE COURAGEOUS

"David also said to Solomon his son, 'Be strong and courageous, and do the work. Do not be afraid or discouraged, for the LORD God, my God, is with you. He will not fail you or forsake you until all the work for the service of the temple of the LORD is finished.'"
1 Chronicles 28:20

It was one of the finest moments in Olympic history: the women's gymnastics finals at the 1996 summer games. Kerri Strug was ready to complete the final rotation on the final day of team competition. Believing that the American team's hopes of victory rested on her, she chose to perform one final vault—despite having suffered a third-degree sprain in her left ankle.

Showing great courage, she said a quick prayer, took a deep breath, and performed the vault to near perfection. She landed on both feet before collapsing in pain. The Americans took home the gold. At only 18 years old, Kerri became a symbol of courage and hope around the world.

The Bible is filled with stories of courage as inspirational as Kerri's. In our verse, David encourages his son Solomon to be strong and courageous. David reminds Solomon that God is with him and will not fail him or forsake him. Even when he's tempted to be afraid or discouraged, Solomon must look to God and trust him for more courage.

We all need courage—to face the day, to take the test, to try out for the play, to deal with a difficult friend. Be a woman of courage today by looking to the Lord to help you.

REFLECT

When you are facing a difficult task and are unsure, take a deep breath, and employ Kerri's prayer: "Come on, God, let me do this one vault." Your "vault" can be anything that requires your utmost courage.

BE HUMBLE

"When someone invites you to a wedding feast, do not take the place of honor, for a person more distinguished than you may have been invited. If so, the host who invited both of you will come and say to you, 'Give this person your seat.' . . . But when you are invited, take the lowest place, so that when your host comes, he will say to you, 'Friend, move up to a better place.' Then you will be honored in the presence of all the other guests. For all those who exalt themselves will be humbled, and those who humble themselves will be exalted."

Luke 14:8-11

Sometimes it feels like God's way is backward—there's something a little weird about it. Teachings like "turn the other cheek," "the last will go first," and "pray for those who hurt you" are the opposite of messages we see all over social media and TV.

Take this verse, for example. The passage is one that sounds so foreign in today's world. Jesus talks about how to act when you go to a wedding reception. Rather than take the best seat at the best table, Christ says to sit in the back instead. Allow the host to invite you to a better table or a better seat.

We live in a culture that encourages you to brag, make yourself the center of attention, and demand your own way. But in this Scripture, Jesus provides an example of how we can humble ourselves in order to allow God to exalt us.

Of course, you should continue to work hard and do your best—but, rather than doing it all for yourself, do it for others and for the glory of God. If you trust him and place your life in his hands, he'll open up all sorts of amazing possibilities in your life.

REFLECT

Are you tempted to push your way to the top? Take the best seat? Demand your way? How might God bless you if you humble yourself and let him direct you?

GOD THE FATHER

"The Spirit you received does not make you slaves, so that you live in fear again; rather, the Spirit you received brought about your adoption to sonship. And by him we cry, '*Abba*, Father.'"

Romans 8:15

There are all kinds of earthly fathers. Perhaps you're lucky enough to have a close relationship with your dad. Or maybe you feel like you hardly know him.

If you lost your dad, due to distance, estrangement, or death, my prayer is that you have a supportive community to lift you up when you need guidance and care. You've probably dealt (or maybe you're still dealing) with a lot of complicated feelings, and I encourage you to talk them out with a friend or older person with whom you feel comfortable speaking your mind.

No matter what your relationship with your earthly dad is like, your heavenly Father is the ultimate father. He's amazing. He's kind, merciful, loving, and faithful. And he adores you. In fact, he loves you so much that he sent Jesus to die for you. Jesus's death brought about your adoption as one of his daughters. You are his precious child, and he loves you. In Scripture, we are invited to call him "Abba," which means "Father."

REFLECT

Why not look up to heaven today and talk to your heavenly dad? He's crazy about you and he loves to hear your voice!

BROKENNESS IS MESSY

"The LORD is close to the brokenhearted and saves those who are crushed in spirit."
Psalm 34:18

Brokenness is messy. My office desk and chair sit on a big glass mat that allows my chair's wheels to roll smoothly. One day, it shattered into a million pieces. There was glass everywhere, and there is nothing neat or tidy about broken glass. As I began to try to clean up the pieces, I was overwhelmed. Mangled sections of glass lay all over the floor. Broom and dustpan in hand, I began to sweep up the fragments. For what seemed like hours, I worked to gather up every single shard. Before it was over, I was drenched in sweat and my hands were scratched and cut.

Neither is there anything simple about broken hearts. One phone call, one conversation, one text, one email can completely wreck our worlds.

I'll bet you know what it's like to have a broken heart. In fact, everyone you know is either going into a hard time, in the middle of one, or coming out of one. Life is filled with pain. In our fallen world, we will all have seasons that crush our spirits and break our hearts.

In those seasons, the Bible tells us that God is near to us. It's when we're in the most pain that Father God is nearest. He steps in and saves us when our spirits are crushed.

REFLECT

Have you had your spirit crushed? Your heart broken? Welcome God's nearness in these hard times and let him in.

GOD SINGS OVER YOU

"The LORD your God is with you, the Mighty Warrior who saves. He will take great delight in you; in his love he will no longer rebuke you, but will rejoice over you with singing."
Zephaniah 3:17

We've all seen that movie in which the hero tries to win a girl's heart by serenading her. You know, the one where he throws pebbles at her window. When she opens it, he cues the band or starts belting out a song while playing his guitar.

It's a romantic gesture. My husband has a beautiful tenor voice, and he's sung to me many times. At our wedding, he sang to me in front of all our friends and family. It was a beautiful moment that I won't ever forget.

Can I tell you something even more beautiful? God sings to you and to me. God is with us, he saves us, he delights in us, and he sings over us with great joy.

The Creator of this universe is singing over you and to you. When you're nervous, you can cue the "God" soundtrack. When you're afraid, God's melody can calm your heart. When you feel alone, he's right beside you, singing a message of hope. You never have to walk alone.

REFLECT

As you go through your day—no matter what comes your way—remember that Father God is with you and singing over you. Can you hear him?

MEDICINE FOR THE HEART

"A cheerful heart is good medicine, but a crushed spirit dries up the bones."
Proverbs 17:22

The Bible talks about heart medicine, but it's not a capsule or pill. In Proverbs 17, we learn that a cheerful heart is good medicine.

Do you have a cheerful heart—one that's happy, joyful, and glad? What does that look like? It's not something you can fake. Great joy comes from pressing in close to Jesus and allowing him to fill your life with peace and purpose. This joy acts like medicine for your heart—raising your spirits and giving you hope.

Conversely, we learn that a crushed or depressed spirit "dries up your bones." That's just God's way of reminding you that deep sadness can make you feel weak or sick. When you're really sad for a long time, it begins to take its toll on your body. You might lose weight, strength, and vitality.

The best medicine for your heart is joy in Christ. If you're feeling sad or depressed for a long period of time, though, talk to your parents, teacher, or another adult with whom you feel comfortable. God does not want you to suffer, and you can get help to feel better.

REFLECT

What makes your heart feel cheerful? How can you seek out more of this each day? If you are struggling with overwhelming thoughts and you need help right away, contact the Crisis Text Line by texting HOME to 741741.

WHAT'S HEAVEN LIKE?

"He will wipe every tear from their eyes. There will be no more death or mourning or crying or pain, for the old order of things has passed away."
Revelation 21:4

What do you think heaven will be like? We all wonder this from time to time. Honestly, the Bible doesn't give us much detail about heaven. It actually says more about what *won't* be there than what will.

Scripture tells us that there will be no more sadness, death, cancer, or pain. Nothing evil or cruel or ugly. There will be no conflicts or arguments. No one will get a divorce. No loss. No hurt. No rejection.

In heaven, we won't worry about what other people think of us. There won't be any filters, hashtags, or likes. You won't worry about things like being popular or wearing the "right" clothes.

Once we're with Jesus, everything will change. You can be certain that heaven is going to be an amazing place. Jesus himself has been preparing it for us, and it's going to be beautiful beyond imagination. We'll be face-to-face with Jesus, freed from sin and death, surrounded by other believers, and filled with incredible joy.

REFLECT

Think about the most gorgeous place you've ever visited. Where was it and what made it special? Consider that heaven will be even better.

DON'T BE DERAILED

"I can do all this through him who gives me strength."
Philippians 4:13

Taking a test. Trying out for the team. Dealing with a difficult friend. Divorce affecting your family. Sharing your faith. Speaking up in class. All of these are common causes of fear.

Many of our fears are legitimate. But we don't have to allow fear to keep us from enjoying life or doing great things. The voice of fear is a liar and you don't have to listen to it. As we learn in Philippians, we can do all things through Christ who gives us strength. Sometimes, we have to walk up to what scares us most and do it anyway. We might do it nervously—but it's still worth it to try.

As a teenager, I sensed God calling me to ministry. Specifically, I felt that God wanted me to write for, and speak to, women—encouraging them and offering them hope. I was nervous about public speaking, and about moving forward in this path of life, but I did it anyway, often with my hands shaking and clammy.

Today, I speak and write to women around the globe. I'm so glad I didn't let fear derail God's plans for my life.

REFLECT

So, what would you do today if you weren't afraid? I dare you to try it—even if you're scared. Ask God to calm your heart.

MEAN GIRLS

"Do not be afraid. Stand firm and you will see the deliverance the LORD will bring you today. . . .The LORD will fight for you; you need only to be still."
Exodus 14:13-14

Mean girls aren't just in movies. They're everywhere: in schools, in churches, in neighborhoods, on cheer squads, in youth groups, on soccer teams, and in the band. The world is full of mean girls, and you've likely met some of them. It's possible you've been hurt by one of them, as well.

What can you do if there are mean girls hurting you? How can you keep them from getting under your skin?

The Bible encourages us to not be afraid of them. Don't let them get to you. Hold your head high and stand tall. You don't have to fight, but you don't have to allow them to push you around, either. Pray for them and let God fight for you. This seems counterintuitive, but God is able to take care of the mean girls and bullies in your life.

It's probably best to put as much distance between you and these girls as possible. It may not be easy, especially if the girls are in your class or part of your friend group. But for your own peace of mind, it's important for you to create distance.

It's also important for you to tell someone what's happening. Talk to a trusted friend, a parent, or a teacher. It's not snitching, and there's no shame in asking for help. Bullying is always unacceptable.

REFLECT

Have you ever been hurt by a group of mean girls? Is the bullying still happening? If so, I encourage you to talk about the situation with someone you trust today. Don't wait!

MONUMENTS OF GOD'S LOVE

"Joshua set up the twelve stones that had been in the middle of the Jordan at the spot where the priests who carried the ark of the covenant had stood. And they are there to this day."

Joshua 4:9

God parted the waters of the Jordan River so the children of Israel could cross over on dry land. While they walked, Joshua recognized the miracle that was taking place. So he told the people to set up 12 huge rocks on the shores of the river to remember the miracle that had taken place. These were like special monuments built to commemorate God's faithfulness. Each time the people saw the stones, they vividly remembered that God takes care of his people.

Today, monuments to God's faithfulness might look a little different. In our house, we have photos that remind us of special events. When our children were baptized, we took pictures and hung them up. When they graduated from high school, we hung their diplomas up, too.

In my own personal collection, I have ceramic figures that I've received as gifts to celebrate special occasions. When I graduated from seminary, a friend gave me the figurine that represents "learning." As I look at my collection, I'm reminded of so many great memories and of the faithfulness of God.

REFLECT

What monuments to God's faithfulness are displayed in your home? Use pictures, certificates, or other items that encourage you to remember that God has blessed you.

PATIENCE

"Be completely humble and gentle; be patient, bearing with one another in love."
Ephesians 4:2

Each day, we have the opportunity to do something powerful—in the carpool line, in class, at the movies with friends, or at home with our families. What is this thing? It's patience—bearing with other people in grace and in love.

Offering patience to those around us can be difficult. We often feel irritated at people for being slow, clueless, and distracted. Our friends and family members don't always think like we do or act like we wish they would. Just like us, they struggle, hurt, and make mistakes, and they need our understanding and gentleness.

So, how patient are you with other people? When you get stuck in line, how do you respond? When your friend is running late (again), how do you react? If your coach keeps you much longer at practice than expected, do you complain? When your parents ask you to stay at the table after dinner to talk, what's your response?

To be more patient, try these ideas: First, take several deep breaths when you feel your impatience mounting. Second, try to see the whole picture. Is there something causing your friend to be late, or impacting your parents right now? Third, when you do respond, try to treat others the way you'd like to be treated if the roles were reversed.

REFLECT

Are you patient with other people? When someone offends or annoys you, be gentle with them. Consider compassion.

YOU CAN BE SAVED

"For it is with your heart that you believe and are justified, and it is with your mouth that you profess your faith and are saved. As Scripture says, 'Anyone who believes in him will never be put to shame.' For there is no difference between Jew and Gentile—the same LORD is LORD of all and richly blesses all who call on him, for, 'Everyone who calls on the name of the LORD will be saved.'"

Romans 10:10-13

If you've been in the church for any length of time, you've likely heard your pastor or youth minister talking about salvation or being born again. Perhaps you've wondered what all this meant. How does a person get saved and give their life to Jesus Christ?

I like to explain salvation using ABC. "A" means *admitting* that you're a sinner. In Romans 3:23, we read that "all have sinned and fall short of the glory of God." I'm a sinner. You're a sinner. The best people you know are sinners. All of us have sinned and need a Savior.

"B" means *believing* in the Lord Jesus Christ as your Savior. Because of our sin, we are all separated from Father God. But Jesus made a way for us to get to God when he died on the cross. Put simply, we can call on the name of the Lord to be saved.

Finally, the "C" in the plan of salvation involves *confession.* There's something incredibly powerful about letting someone know about your decision to trust Christ. If you've made that decision, tell your parents or youth pastor. They'll be so excited for you!

REFLECT

Have you accepted the gift of salvation? Have you admitted your sin and believed Jesus can save you? Who will you tell about your decision?

NOTHING CAN SEPARATE YOU FROM GOD

"No, in all these things we are more than conquerors through him who loved us. For I am convinced that neither death nor life, neither angels nor demons, neither the present nor the future, nor any powers, neither height nor depth, nor anything else in all creation, will be able to separate us from the love of God that is in Christ Jesus our LORD."
Romans 8:37-39

Unquestionably, it was one of the scariest days of my life. My children were very small—my daughter was a baby and my son was about three years old. We were playing at a park on a gorgeous spring day. One minute, my son was playing with some other boys on the slide—the next minute, he was gone.

I went into intense Mom Mode, hunting all over the park for my little guy. Nothing was going to separate me from my firstborn. Frantically, I searched everywhere, before finally finding my son playing with his cars in a large ditch, completely oblivious to the whole ordeal.

God, your heavenly parent, promises that nothing can separate you from his love—not life, death, angels, demons . . . he won't let anything come between you. He loves you totally and completely. If you pull away—or just wander off into a ditch to play—he will come looking for you.

REFLECT

How does it feel to know that you'll never be separated from God's love?

TWO ARE BETTER THAN ONE

"Two are better than one, because they have a good return for their labor: If either of them falls down, one can help the other up. But pity anyone who falls and has no one to help them up."

Ecclesiastes 4:9-10

If you've ever run a three-legged race, you know how difficult it is. If you and your partner get into a rhythm, your three legs can move quickly. However, if you run out of sync, you usually fall over.

Certainly, individuals can accomplish much on their own, but often two people can do more—especially when they work together.

For example, I'm one of those women who likes to walk fast, and I love to have a friend walk with me. To walk with someone else is to walk faster, farther, and with more enjoyment.

Everyone needs people to walk through life with them. We all need friends who will stand by us, walk alongside us, and pick us up when we fall down. We need people who will support us, pray for us, and encourage us in the race of life. You and I were not created to walk alone.

REFLECT

Name three or four friends who walk with you in life. What do you appreciate most about these friends? If you're still searching for a friend like that, that's okay, too. Pray and ask God to send you someone who will walk beside you.

GETTING BAD NEWS

"They will have no fear of bad news; their hearts are steadfast, trusting in the LORD."
Psalm 112:7

Bad news comes without warning into everyone's life. When was the last time you heard bad news? Maybe you got a bad grade on a test, or perhaps you found out that you hadn't been invited to a party. Bad news could be your boyfriend telling you he wanted to break up. Whatever form it takes, it's not easy to hear.

Here's the good news about bad news: It doesn't have to destroy you. Your heart can be steadfast, trusting in the Lord. No matter what comes your way, you can handle it. How? Try the "catch, double-check, deal, and heal" method.

When the news comes in, first you must "catch" it. Make sure you heard it all and heard it right.

Then, double-check the information. Talk to the person who delivered the news and make sure you didn't misunderstand it.

Next, you must deal with the bad news. Allow yourself time to process, feel, and grasp the emotional impact of what you heard. Give yourself time to grieve through the pain.

Finally, believe that you *will* heal. It may take time, but you will survive whatever comes your way. Trust in the Lord and ask him to make you stronger as you work through the pain or anger.

REFLECT

Had any bad news lately? What was it, and how did you deal with it? Use the "catch, double-check, deal, and heal" method and consider how it works for you.

DECLARE YOUR FAITH

"But in your hearts revere Christ as LORD. Always be prepared to give an answer to everyone who asks you to give the reason for the hope that you have. But do this with gentleness and respect."

1 Peter 3:15

If you were put on the spot and asked to share your faith today, could you do it? Could you answer a classmate, friend, or even a stranger who asked why you believe in Jesus? In this verse, Peter encourages us to always be ready to give an answer to anyone who asks. You and I need to be prepared to share our faith in Christ with gentleness and respect.

Recently, one of my friends was at the local gas station. The man at the pump next to her surprised her by asking what she was witnessing. My friend was confused, unsure why he was asking her this. He pointed at her T-shirt, which boldly displayed the word "witness."

Realizing what was happening, my friend was able to briefly share her faith in Christ, even though the man's question had caught her off guard. Although she was able to share a little, she admitted that she wasn't really prepared to share her faith that day.

It's so easy to display a Jesus bumper sticker or wear a Christian T-shirt. What's not so easy is feeling ready to share the gospel when someone asks. Sharing doesn't have to be profound or lengthy, and we can do some preparation in advance by thinking through the reasons why we have hope in our Savior.

REFLECT

Have you ever had anyone ask you to share your faith? If so, how did it go? If not, take a few moments to decide what you'd say if someone asked you about Christ.

HOW TO BE BLESSED

"Blessed is the one who does not walk in step with the wicked or stand in the way that sinners take or sit in the company of mockers, but whose delight is in the law of the LORD, and who meditates on his law day and night. That person is like a tree planted by streams of water, which yields its fruit in season and whose leaf does not wither—whatever they do prospers."

Psalm 1:1-3

Would you like to be blessed? Happier? More fulfilled? The Bible talks a great deal about how to make this happen. One of the most fascinating chapters is found in the first Psalm.

Psalm 1 tells us that we are blessed if we don't walk alongside people who are wicked. What does that look like in your life? The wicked are those who always push you to do things that feel wrong or questionable—things that hurt you or others, or damage your relationships with other people. Those who are wicked pull you away from what is good.

Psalm 1 also says you should avoid sitting with people who mock the gospel. Of course, you can have friends who don't know Christ. In fact, it's healthy to know people who are different from you. But if a friend regularly makes fun of you and mocks your faith, they'll pull you down.

Finally, Psalm 1 tells us we'll be blessed when we make a big deal out of the Bible. Read it, memorize some verses, write out your thoughts in your journal, and focus on it in the morning and at night. When you and I study the Bible, God will bless us. He'll build us into strong, flourishing trees with leaves that won't wither.

REFLECT

Have you had to avoid certain people at school or church because of the way they pull you toward evil? How have you handled this?

AS WISE AS YOUR TEACHERS

"I have more insight than all my teachers, for I meditate on your statutes."
Psalm 119:99

I remember the first time I read this verse. I was in high school, and it blew me away. I could have more insights and wisdom than all my teachers just by meditating on, studying, and learning God's word. That sounded pretty good to me!

One great lesson on how to meditate on the Bible comes from cows. Yes, I'm serious. Cows chew their food all the time: up to eight hours of chewing every day.

It might sound weird, but that's exactly what we're supposed to do with the Bible. We read it in the morning. Then, we chew on it all day long. Over and over, we bring it back to our minds and ponder it. We think about a verse and ask ourselves, "What does it mean? How can I apply it to my life?"

If you chew on the food of the Word, you'll be wise and have more insights than you ever thought possible.

REFLECT

How often do you meditate on the Bible? Try to read at least one verse a day and reflect on what you learned from it.

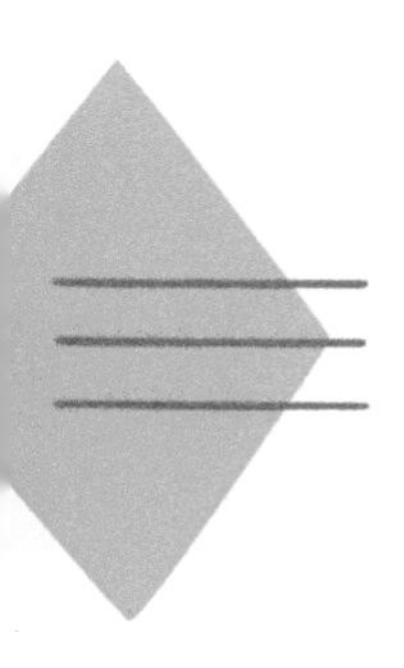

WALKING WITH INTEGRITY

"Whoever walks in integrity walks securely,
but whoever takes crooked paths will be found out."
Proverbs 10:9

On a hike with my family, we came to a fork in the road. Both paths ultimately led to the same destination, but we had to select one or the other. To the left was a narrow, almost hidden, path; it looked steep and rocky. It would be faster, but the signs posted near it warned that it was dangerous. To the right was a wider path; it looked more level and easier to climb. We ultimately chose the path to the right.

Life is filled with paths to choose, and we come to forks in the road on a regular basis. You may not be selecting a hiking trail, but you'll likely have to make many decisions throughout this day. For instance, you'll have to choose what to wear, what to eat, what to pack for school, where to sit at lunch, how to spend your time after school, and how long to spend on your homework. How can you make the best choices—even in small things?

In Scripture, we learn that walking securely means acting with integrity. Integrity helps us make better choices. But what *is* integrity? Simply put, it's who we are in the deepest places of our heart. Integrity is honesty. It's good character. It's being truthful and real. It's authenticity.

REFLECT

Are you a person of integrity and character? How have you seen honesty and truthfulness pay off in your life or in the lives of others? How has integrity helped you make better choices?

NAVIGATING STRONG EMOTIONS

"Better a patient person than a warrior, one with self-control than one who takes a city."
Proverbs 16:32

It's all too easy to let strong emotions get the best of us. Anger, fear, worry, doubt, anxiety, and rage can affect us mentally and emotionally.

The Bible encourages us to be patient and practice self-control. It's important to nurture our ability to govern our emotions, our speech, and our reactions when things upset us.

How do you deal with strong emotions? Do you stuff them down deep inside? When you're angry or hurt, do you blow up? Or do you let things simmer until they boil over?

One way you can gain better control over your emotions is to pray about them. Talk to God about each irritation and each situation that's upsetting you. Invite him to make you a more patient, calm, and self-controlled person—no matter what comes your way.

Expressing or processing our emotions can be so hard, and many, many people struggle to do so. If you're finding it extra difficult and you need some help, call or text a friend, or tell your parents or an adult at school or church. They can help you talk your feelings out and recommend steps for you to take toward healing.

REFLECT

Recite to yourself a list of the "buttons" you know you have—the tender parts that can provoke emotions. Think about how you've seen other people react to the same stress points and how their reactions differ from yours.

FORGIVENESS

"Then Peter came to Jesus and asked, 'LORD, how many times shall I forgive my brother or sister who sins against me? Up to seven times?' Jesus answered, 'I tell you, not seven times, but seventy-seven times.'"

Matthew 18:21-22

We all have people in our lives who can hurt us—and the betrayals of good friends, whether purposeful or accidental, can hurt our hearts the most.

Maybe you've been there: You hoped to spend time with a friend, but they paid attention to someone else. You found out about a party or social event you weren't invited to, and you felt rejected and mistreated. Relationships are tricky and prickly and can often be hurtful.

So what should we do when someone hurts us or lets us down? In the Gospel of Matthew, Peter asked Jesus how many times he should forgive the same person, hoping that Jesus would provide a limit. Jesus told him he must forgive that person 77 times—but by that time, Peter would likely lose count. So it's easy to see what Jesus meant: We should forgive over and over again, without limit. Even when we'd rather not, we must continue to show grace to our friends and family by forgiving them.

REFLECT

Think of someone who hurt you lately. Have you forgiven them? If not, pray to God to change your heart and open it to forgiveness.

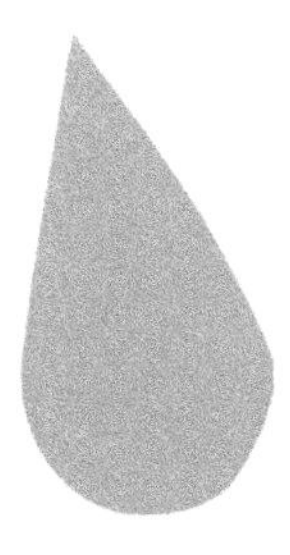

THAT'S WHY IT'S CALLED GRACE

"And if by grace, then it cannot be based on works; if it were, grace would no longer be grace."
Romans 11:6

I was once driving to church when I went through a four-way stop too quickly. The blue lights of a police car began to flash in my rearview mirror.

As the young police officer approached my car, I knew I had messed up. I handed over my driver's license and registration, and he asked me if I realized that I hadn't come to a complete stop. I acknowledged that I may have rolled through a bit too quickly.

He took my credentials and went back to his patrol car. After a few moments, he came back to my window and asked me where I was headed. I told him, and was surprised when he patted the roof of my car, told me to be more careful, and wished me a good day. I drove off without a ticket!

It was all grace.

Grace is that moment when you receive a gift you feel you don't deserve. It's when you expect punishment but get forgiveness instead. It's not based on works, actions, or being a nice person. Grace is what God gives us through the person of Jesus Christ, who brought about grace by his death and resurrection.

REFLECT

Have you recently received a gift you felt you didn't deserve? Think of a time when God showered your life with grace.

GROWING INTO AN ADULT

"Don't let anyone look down on you because you are young, but set an example for the believers in speech, in conduct, in love, in faith, and in purity."
1 Timothy 4:12

Do you ever feel like people look down on you or treat you like you're still a kid? Do they try to discourage you from doing the things you care about, just because you're young?

Don't let your age keep you from doing what God has made you to do. In the Bible, Paul told Timothy this very thing. He exhorted Timothy not to pay attention to people who looked down on him. Instead, Paul wanted him to set an example for others in the way he talked and lived.

So what can you do to set an example? Write that book you've been wanting to write. Paint that painting. Write that song and sing it with your choir. Volunteer to share a devotional. Offer to coach or mentor a younger student. Step out in faith and use the gifts God has given you. Don't let anyone tell you that you can't!

REFLECT

Are you letting your age hold you back? If you were older, what would you try? Take one small step toward that dream today.

HELPING OTHERS

"Give, and it will be given to you. A good measure, pressed down, shaken together and running over, will be poured into your lap. For with the measure you use, it will be measured to you."

Luke 6:38

As believers, we can choose how much to give, what to give, and how often to give. It's completely up to us.

I like to categorize giving into four sizes, from small to jumbo. Small gifts of service might include sending a text to a hurting friend or writing them an encouraging note. Or you can give a little money or a few items of clothes to those in need.

Medium types of service could be helping at a soup kitchen, babysitting for free, or walking the dog without being asked.

To serve in larger ways, you might sign up for a volunteer day, read to a group of kids, give a larger amount of money to a cause you love, or donate a big stack of clothes. If you want to do some jumbo-size service, sign up for a mission trip or project. Or save your money for a whole year and make a large donation to a cause that's close to your heart.

In the Bible, Jesus says that when we give, we'll receive gifts in return. The size of the gift you give is the same size that's returned to you. Give generously and God will pour good things into your life.

REFLECT

What category of giving fits best into your life right now? Be honest about your time, resources, and abilities. Then spend at least five minutes doing research into one way you could practice giving.

TAKE EVERY THOUGHT CAPTIVE

"We demolish arguments and every pretension that sets itself up against the knowledge of God, and we take captive every thought to make it obedient to Christ."

2 Corinthians 10:5

Some moments in life are unforgettable. At my high school, the senior class always pulled a prank at the end of the year. One year, a group of guys bought live crickets, which they let loose in school early one morning. Crickets were chirping in the classrooms, in the lunchroom, at chapel, everywhere.

All day, teachers encouraged us to catch those crickets wherever we could. It was one of the funniest days I remember in high school—the day the crickets took over. But the ones that escaped capture haunted the halls for weeks—chirping away.

Negative, discouraging, and worrisome thoughts can feel a lot like those crickets. They hop around in your head all day, loudly and persistently. So how can you catch and release them before they take over your life?

Here are a few ways to take your thoughts captive: First, notice what you're thinking about. Is it negative, hurtful, or self-defeating? Next, capture that thought and resolve to deal with it. Finally, replace that negative thought with a positive one. Focus on a Scripture verse or an encouraging quote.

REFLECT

Do you struggle with your thoughts? What thoughts do you need to capture right now? Concentrate on replacing the bad thoughts with positive intentions. Think about a favorite Bible verse or the words to an encouraging song.

DIGITAL CLEANSE

"'I have the right to do anything,' you say—but not everything is beneficial. 'I have the right to do anything'—but not everything is constructive."

1 Corinthians 10:23

The concept of taking a "digital break" is trendy these days. That's when you put aside every device that has a screen: your tablet, TV, cell phone, and computer. During the break, you do things you've been missing: read books, talk to friends and family, exercise, and get outside.

It's so easy to spend hours a day on your phone and other devices. And it may feel like we're connecting with people that way. But social media can actually make your life lonelier. When consumed with everyone else's life, we forget to live our own. We have to remember not to let all of our relationships and interactions exist online. It's good to be with real people—looking them in the eyes and hearing their voices.

According to the Bible, we have the right to do most things. However, some are not constructive. It may feel good to spend time growing your Instagram account and watching the latest Netflix original show—but every so often, it can be a relief to step back and consider whether taking a break might help you rest or gain a new perspective on your relationships.

REFLECT

Take a digital break for a day or a week. That means no phone, computer, social media, Netflix, or Hulu. After your break, reflect: Did you go bonkers? Or did you find the time away to be refreshing? Consider incorporating the positive parts of a digital break into your everyday life.

STEP INTO THE NEW

"Forget the former things; do not dwell on the past. See, I am doing a new thing! Now it springs up; do you not perceive it? I am making a way in the wilderness and streams in the wasteland."
Isaiah 43:18-19

I like new things. New clothes. New shoes. New people. There's something about the freshness, the unexpected, and the unknown that surprises me and adds variety to my life.

Guess what? God loves new things, too. In fact, he does new things all the time. He's constantly sending new people into your life and opening new doors for you to walk through.

What new things is God doing in your life right now? Has he invited you to do something you've never done before? It doesn't have to be huge. Sometimes even the smallest changes can change our perspective. You could order something at your favorite restaurant that you've never tried before. Or you could walk a new way to class or drive a new way to school.

Maybe God is sending you a new friend, a new opportunity, a new idea, or a new ministry. Will you step out of your comfort zone and step into the new? To continue to grow and succeed, we must sometimes be willing to follow God down new paths.

REFLECT

Is God calling you to try something new? Will you go for it? If not, what's holding you back? Try visualizing what great things could happen if you have the courage to follow God's prompts.

WAIT ON GOD

"I remain confident of this: I will see the goodness of the LORD in the land of the living. Wait for the LORD; be strong and take heart and wait for the LORD."
Psalm 27:13-14

The Bible frequently mentions waiting on God. To wait on God is to be confident that he will show up—no matter how grave our situation may appear to be. To wait on God is to believe that he will be good to us and take care of us.

But waiting on God is *hard.* It's not for the faint-hearted. We must be strong and tell our hearts to be courageous, even when we're tempted to give up.

The Bible is filled with stories of people who waited on God and were richly rewarded: Abraham and Sarah waited 25 years to welcome a baby boy. Joseph labored for 13 years in slavery before being promoted to Pharaoh's second in command. Moses waited 40 years before God called him to save the Israelites. Jesus waited 30 years before starting his earthly ministry.

So what are you waiting on God to do? Does it seem like he's taking a long time? Maybe you're waiting on him to provide for your family, restore a relationship, or heal an illness. Maybe you've been praying the same request for several years with no answer.

Whatever the case, wait on the Lord. Be strong. Tell your heart to be courageous. Remind yourself of all that God has done for you in the past. Remember the ways he's taken care of you. God is good, and you will experience his goodness soon.

REFLECT

What are you waiting for God to do? What are two or three ways you can encourage your own heart and boost your courage?

FITTING IN

"Am I now trying to win the approval of human beings, or of God? Or am I trying to please people? If I were still trying to please people, I would not be a servant of Christ."
Galatians 1:10

When my daughter was in 10th grade, she moved to a new school. There was a group of girls who all sat together at lunch. They were the most popular girls, and my daughter wanted to be included in their group.

Finally, the day came when they invited Emily to sit with them. She was so excited—she was finally being included. But she soon found out that although they were beautiful and popular, they were not the warm, welcoming friends she needed. Emily was disappointed—all that time she'd spent trying to win the approval of these girls was wasted.

In this verse, the Apostle Paul sums up Emily's predicament, and the predicaments of so many young women like her: Are you living to win God's approval or the approval of other people? You can't live your life to please both people and God. You must choose one or the other. You can either spend all of your time trying to get people to like you and include you—or you can rest in God's loving embrace.

There is only one person we should spend our lives trying to please. He is our Father God.

REFLECT

Are you trying to get a particular person or group of people to like or accept you? Spend a few minutes thinking about their qualities. Are they living the kind of lives that will bring you closer to God?

FAITHFUL PEOPLE

"Whoever can be trusted with very little can also be trusted with much, and whoever is dishonest with very little will also be dishonest with much."
Luke 16:10

I heard a story years ago about a young woman who was looking for a job. At one store, the manager had a task for anyone who wanted to be considered: sort a huge container of nails and paper clips into separate boxes.

She worked diligently, pulling out all of the paper clips and putting them into a box. Then she moved all of the nails into a second box. When the work was complete, she discovered a $100 bill in the bottom of the original container.

When she was finished, she handed over the money and told the manager that the job was done. The manager handed the $100 back to her—a reward for being persistent, hardworking, and honest—and hired her on the spot.

To be trusted with hard work, odd jobs, and boring tasks—it's all part of being responsible and faithful. This verse teaches us that the person who can be trusted with little things can also be trusted with more serious tasks.

REFLECT

Are you a faithful and responsible person? Can you be trusted with the little things as well as the big?

LOVE WHEN YOU'RE READY

"Daughters of Jerusalem, I charge you: Do not arouse or awaken love until it so desires."
Song of Solomon 8:4

Brownies are my specialty, and they're best straight from the oven. But, every once in a while, I accidentally pull the brownies out of the oven too early. I'll bite into one to find that it's undercooked, soupy, and disappointing. I've found that I have to stick a toothpick in the brownies as they bake in order to test whether or not they are ready.

This verse from the Song of Solomon also addresses the theme of being ready—in this case, being ready to fall in love, and handling the intense emotions and desires that come along with that.

The verse encourages the daughters of Jerusalem not to arouse or awaken love until the time is right. When you have a crush that turns into dating, and then a relationship, it's so exciting and fun. As you enjoy the new feelings and closeness, it's important to know where your boundaries are when it comes to physical affection.

As you move into middle school, high school, and college, the boys get cuter and the temptations get stronger. As a young woman, you have to guard your heart from falling for every guy that smiles at you. Save your love, your affection, and your heart for the best guy.

A healthy sexual relationship is best when saved for marriage; that's the way God designed it to be. A great guy won't pressure or manipulate you to have sex before you're ready. You get to decide when, where, and how intimacy will happen in your life.

REFLECT

How can you express your affection for a romantic partner while respecting God's plan for you? This might be a great topic to bring up with your mom, an older sister, or a trusted older friend.

WORTH MORE THAN GOLD

"How much better to get wisdom than gold, to get insight rather than silver!"
Proverbs 16:16

If I asked you to describe your school, what would you tell me? Is it located in a traditional setting or are you homeschooled? Is it massive and filled with tons of kids or small and more subdued? Do you have to wear uniforms? Are there lots of great teachers, extracurricular activities, and people?

Even if you enjoy it, you probably have mixed feelings about it sometimes. There may be classes and subjects that you love and excel in. Others might be boring, and you won't use the lessons as much. Despite this, learning is never a waste of time. You can learn from every teacher, in every class, and in every situation. When you're learning, you're growing into a more well-rounded person who can think critically.

The Bible tells us that it's better to get wisdom than gold, and better to gain insight instead of silver. In a culture that worships money as the ultimate goal, this seems like a strange idea. But Scripture makes it clear: A young woman with incredible insights, wisdom, understanding, and grace is richer than one who's loaded with cash but lacks these qualities.

Solomon, the man who penned this verse, had the opportunity to ask God for anything he wanted. He could have asked for money, power, prestige, or fame. Instead, he asked to be made wise and insightful. And God granted his request. Why not ask God to do the same for you? Invite him to make you a wise and insightful young woman.

REFLECT

Who is the wisest person you know? In what ways does their wisdom guide you?

OVERCOME STRESS

"I keep my eyes always on the LORD. With him at my right hand, I will not be shaken. Therefore my heart is glad and my tongue rejoices; my body also will rest secure."
Psalm 16:8-9

Quick—without thinking about it for too long, name four or five things that are stressing you out right now. I'm sure you can easily name a few.

As I was writing this devotion, I had to stop and do something that I regularly do. I got down on my knees and once again laid out my stresses before the Lord.

Stress impacts everyone—young or old, rich or poor, famous or unknown. We all have to learn how to deal with it. Luckily, the Bible tells us how: We must keep our eyes always on the Lord. We fix our eyes on Jesus, knowing he can take care of *all* of our stuff. Recognizing that he's right beside us, we learn to not be shaken. We can find joy and gladness as we rest in him.

After I cried out to the Lord with my stresses, I got up unshaken, calm, and able to face the day. My heart was no longer anxious. Instead, there was great peace.

REFLECT

You can do this as well. Get alone with God and give him your stresses. With his help, you will not be shaken.

MAKE ADJUSTMENTS

"Do not lie to each other, since you have taken off your old self with its practices and have put on the new self, which is being renewed in knowledge in the image of its Creator."
Colossians 3:9-10

My daughter and I can't pass through a department store or mall without stopping to look at shoes. Emily is a self-professed shoe addict. After all, who doesn't love getting a new pair of shoes? But no one warns you of the adjustments that a new pair of heels or sandals may require. Sometimes you have to break them in before you can wear them comfortably without getting blisters.

Believers in Christ have to make some adjustments, too, when we come to faith in him. When you take off your old self and put on a new self, things are different. Your old ways are gone; new disciplines must take their place. Your old habits, ways of thinking, and sometimes even the words you use must be renewed and transformed.

Becoming more like Jesus means accepting renovations. From the time we accept Jesus as our Savior until the time we enter heaven, our hearts and minds are undergoing construction. Not all of the changes will be pleasant, but their goal is beautiful. God is always at work in us—conforming us to look more and more like his Son.

REFLECT

Like breaking in a pair of shoes, replacing your old way of life with a new one can be painful. Life renovations go better when we spend time with friends and other peers who love Jesus. Reading devotions, listening to positive music and podcasts, and getting involved in a good Bible study group can also help.

LOVE YOUR NEIGHBORS

"'The most important one,' answered Jesus, 'is this . . . Love the LORD your God with all your heart and with all your soul and with all your mind and with all your strength. The second is this: Love your neighbor as yourself. There is no commandment greater than these.'"
Mark 12:29-31

The Bible instructs us to love God and to love your neighbor as yourself. And your neighbor is not just the person who lives next door. Your neighbor is the student whose locker is next to yours. Your neighbor is your teammate, classmate, lab partner, and your carpool or bus companions.

Neighbors can also include those in your community. Basically, a neighbor is any person God puts in your sphere of influence—anyone with whom you have some sort of interaction.

How can you love your neighbors better? It's actually quite simple. If you go to a coffee shop, smile at the barista. If you bump into one of your mom's friends at the mall, ask them how they're doing. If a new student starts at your school, be friendly and welcoming.

In the last few days, I've had the opportunity to show kindness to several new neighbors. One shared that she found her job exhausting, and I offered her encouragement. The second asked for career advice, which I was happy to provide. My third encounter was with a young man who'd had his heart broken by his girlfriend. I offered him words of comfort.

REFLECT

Being neighborly isn't hard, but it does require unselfishly giving of your time. To love your neighbor, you could pick up trash in their yard. Or you could share lunch money with a friend at school who forgets their lunch.

GROWING IN WISDOM

"And Jesus grew in wisdom and stature, and in favor with God and man."
Luke 2:52

When I was in seventh grade, I grew six inches. I went from 5'1" to 5'7" in just a few short months. It was as if I grew taller overnight. My clothes didn't fit anymore and I was rather clumsy and awkward. And I noticed that the guys in my class seemed especially short.

You're probably noticing some big changes in your body, too. Often, girls mature and grow taller before guys do. (You may notice a lot of short boys in your class.)

There's not much mention of Jesus's teenage years in the Bible. This one verse basically covers his life as a teen: He grew and increased in wisdom, in stature, and in favor with God and man.

Like Jesus, you're growing in wisdom, too. For example, think about how much you're learning—both emotionally and academically. If I were to ask you to share all of the lessons you've learned in the past month, I'll bet you could give me pages of wisdom.

And you're learning to get along with other people better. Through relationships with coaches, teachers, teammates, classmates, parents, siblings, and more, you're gaining incredible insights about communication and interpersonal skills. What a great time to focus on your relationship with the Lord—to mature, to learn, and to get to know him better, too.

REFLECT

How have you grown this year? What's the most amazing thing you've learned recently—emotionally, physically, spiritually, or in your relationships?

MAKING THE BEST DECISIONS

"Trust in the LORD with all your heart and lean not on your own understanding; in all your ways submit to him, and he will make your paths straight."
Proverbs 3:5-6

Have you ever been faced with a big decision, like deciding whether to try out for a team, go out with a guy, or hang out with a certain group of friends? Maybe you're trying to decide which high school or college to attend.

Big decisions come our way often, so it's helpful to learn how to make them. Do you poll your friends to see what they think? Maybe you talk to your parents or siblings. You may search social media or read a book to see what other people do when faced with the same dilemma.

God's word talks about making the best decisions. As we trust in the Lord with all of our hearts, submitting to his will, he promises to make our paths straight. But what does this really look like?

When my family is faced with a decision that involves multiple options, we use a method we call the "Question at the Top of the Page." We pull out a piece of paper and write our question in a simple "yes/no" format at the top of the page. Then, we begin to pray. In the following days and weeks, we notice every verse, sermon, event, and conversation that could relate to our question. We write down everything that happens underneath our question. Without fail, we come to the best decision by praying about this question until we get an answer.

REFLECT

What's the biggest decision you're facing right now? Try the "Question at the Top of the Page" and see if it helps you.

COMPARISON IS THE THIEF OF ALL JOY

"We do not dare to classify or compare ourselves with some who commend themselves. When they measure themselves by themselves and compare themselves with themselves, they are not wise."
2 Corinthians 10:12

There's a woman at my gym who is just stunning. Perfect hair. Perfect smile. Great style. When my friends and I worked out, we would talk and laugh with each other. She never joined in, and we didn't invite her to. The simple fact is: We felt intimidated.

One day, I felt that the Lord wanted me to talk to her. Honestly, I didn't particularly want to, because I felt so inadequate compared to her. But I couldn't shake the conviction that I should start a conversation.

So I went over to the machines where she was lifting weights and greeted her with something simple, like, "Hey, how are you?"

At first, she seemed startled. Then she smiled and we chatted throughout the entire workout. As I was leaving, she stopped me and said something I've never forgotten. She thanked me for talking to her and told me that no one at the gym had ever spoken to her.

Isn't that crazy? As women, we often compare ourselves to each other and feel like we don't measure up. But you never know what's going on in other people's lives, or what you might be missing while you spend your time comparing.

REFLECT

How can you overcome the temptation to compare yourself to others? Next time you're suffering from feelings of inadequacy, try reaching out to the person who inspired those feelings.

DOING YOUR BEST

"Whatever you do, work at it with all your heart, as working for the LORD, not for human masters, since you know that you will receive an inheritance from the LORD as a reward. It is the LORD Christ you are serving."
Colossians 3:23-24

We all have to do things we'd rather not do. Clean your room. Babysit your younger brother. Write a boring paper for class. Run extra sprints after practice. Play the piece one more time at band practice.

Life is full of mundane tasks. This will be true for the rest of your life. So how do you stay motivated and follow through when you'd rather not? One trick is to think about *why* you do things. Ultimately, your work is for the Lord, not for anyone else.

The Bible encourages us to give our very best. In school, at home, at work—whatever you do—God wants you to work with all of your heart. And he'll reward you for giving your very best.

REFLECT

How do you stay motivated to work hard, even when you don't want to? Brainstorm three ways you can keep going even when you're feeling bored or your energy is lagging.

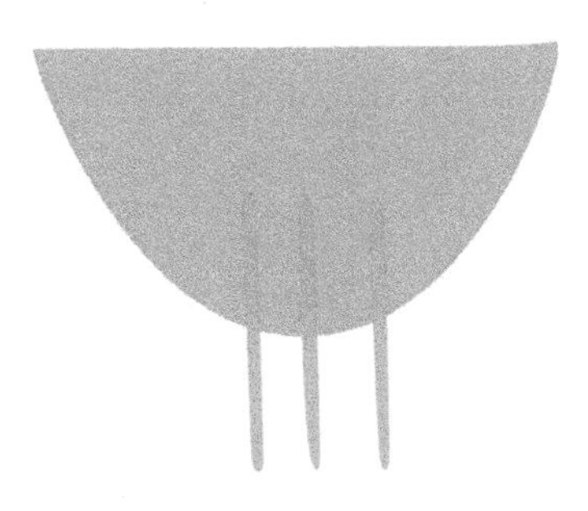

WALKING THROUGH DARKNESS

"Even though I walk through the darkest valley, I will fear no evil, for you are with me; your rod and your staff, they comfort me."

Psalm 23:4

When I was a kid, we had a babysitter who liked to watch a TV show called *Dark Shadows*. I hated it. The characters, the storylines, even the music—everything about it creeped me out.

For many people, shadows, valleys, and the darkness of life are scary. We get nervous when we start talking about these issues.

God's word reminds us that even when you go through dark places, you don't have to fear. You don't have to be nervous. Father God walks with you. His shepherd's rod is there to fight off your enemies. The shepherd's staff has a crook in it that perfectly fits around the neck of a sheep. When sheep get out of line, the shepherd can place the staff around their necks and gently lead them back to the rest of the herd. Similarly, God uses his staff to gently lead us—especially when we get lost in the dark.

Life is filled with joys, like beautiful sunsets, the laughter of little children, beautiful music, and great conversations. There is always light in the midst of dark seasons. Let God show you the way through supportive communities, comforting words of Scripture, and the small delights of the world.

REFLECT

How have you experienced dark valleys in your life? Have you sensed God near you in these valleys? Have you ever felt God's rod or staff directing you?

EXPECT MORE

"Now to him who is able to do immeasurably more than all we ask or imagine, according to his power that is at work within us, to him be glory in the church and in Christ Jesus throughout all generations, for ever and ever! Amen."
Ephesians 3:20-21

A friend once gave me a large wooden sign that says "PRAY BIG" in bold white letters. It's the perfect reminder. In Ephesians, we learn that God is able to do immeasurably more than all we can ask for or dare to imagine. Other translations use words like "far more" and "infinitely more." But do you really believe this? Do you expect more and pray for more?

Today, ask God to do more—immeasurably more—in your life, and see what changes. Pray for bigger things, expect bigger things, and believe bigger things. For example, let's say you really desire to have a good friend. What if you begin to pray for and expect God to send you the best friend you've ever had? Or maybe you're hoping for a part in the school play, to have one of your poems published, or for acceptance to the college of your dreams. Have you prayed about this? Today would be a great day to start!

REFLECT
What's the greatest desire of your heart right now? Pray about it and ask God to do immeasurably more than even what you ask for.

FRIENDS IN FAITH

"Do not be yoked together with unbelievers. For what do righteousness and wickedness have in common? Or what fellowship can light have with darkness?"
2 Corinthians 6:14

Maria is the friend who pushes me to work harder. Sarah calls when she thinks I might need a kind word. Ellie prays for me and my family. Lori makes me laugh at myself—no matter how badly I've blown it.

They are some of my best friends, and each of them makes me a better person in some way. Each of them loves Jesus, loves me, and has a powerful impact on my life.

What about you? Who do you hang out with? Do you have friends who make you a better person?

Scripture teaches us that we need to be careful who we spend time with. The word "yoke" conveys the idea of chaining our lives to someone else's life. If our friends are good and righteous people, being yoked to their lives is a wonderful thing. Positive people can make us more positive; hanging out with godly friends can make us more godly.

However, we have to be careful about spending too much time with those who walk in darkness. It's definitely possible to lead others to Christ by our kindness and friendship. But if your only friends are walking apart from the Lord, they can pull you down, dragging you away from the light and leading you to sin.

As a believer, you are designed to walk in the light. Your most fulfilling and rewarding relationships will be with those who are also walking in the light.

REFLECT

Who are your best friends? How do they make you a better person?

ALL THINGS FOR GOOD

"You intended to harm me, but God intended it for good to accomplish what is now being done, the saving of many lives."
Genesis 50:20

God works in mysterious ways. Although it may sometimes feel like everything is falling apart, God is actually bringing all of the events in your life together for your benefit.

In God's economy, the things that threaten to break us are actually what he uses to help us grow, make us stronger, and take us to new heights. Maybe you're facing a deep hurt or confusing situation. Your parents are splitting up. Your pastor has been asked to step down. You're being bullied. It could be none of these things—regardless, you know what it's like to hurt, because we've all experienced pain at some point in our lives.

Although it may not make sense now, God can take the worst moments of your life and use them to accomplish incredible things. Your greatest misery can become your greatest triumph. God's intentions are always good when it comes to you.

REFLECT

Have you seen God work things for good in your life? How has he saved the day when you thought all was lost?

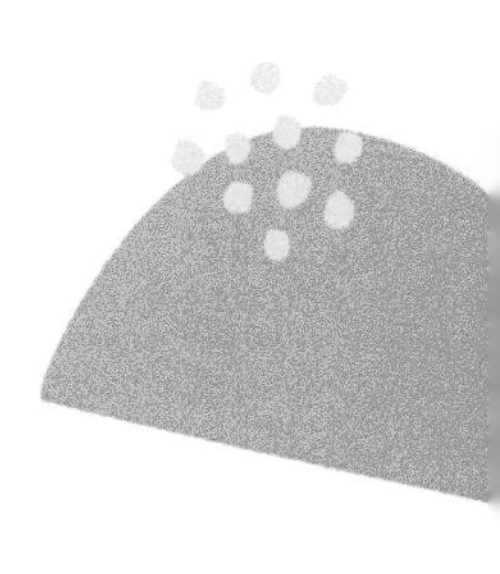

BE HONORABLE

"For we are taking pains to do what is right, not only in the eyes of the LORD but also in the eyes of man."
2 Corinthians 8:21

What does it mean to act honorably? Some call it "taking the high road." Honorable people are principled people, behaving with grace and dignity.

If you're an honorable person, people can count on you. You do what you say you're going to do, when you say you'll do it. You're truthful, fair, and honest. Your friends, family, and teachers would say that you take the high road as often as you can.

In the Bible, Paul reminds the people of the church at Corinth to be honorable, taking pains to do what's right. In other words, work hard at doing well: doing your homework regularly, studying for tests, and showing up for your friends when you say you will. Make it your practice to be well-thought-of in the eyes of God and man.

Why not take the high road? There's plenty of room up there because so few people are on it.

REFLECT

Can you honestly say that you're an honorable person? Think of a time when you've behaved honorably lately. If nothing comes to mind, what could you start doing today to raise the bar in your life?

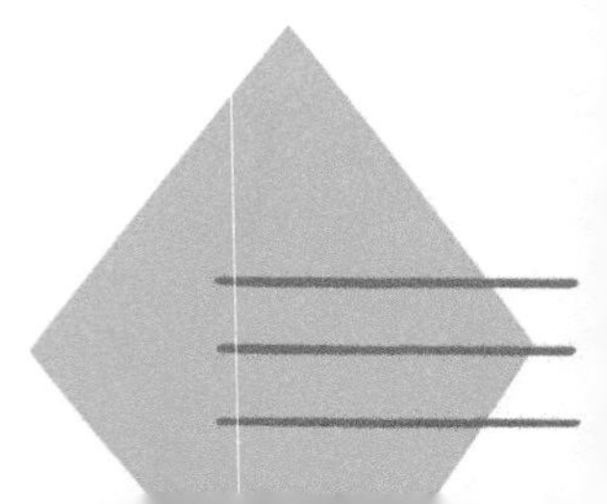

FRIENDS ARE PATIENT; FRIENDS ARE KIND

"Love is patient, love is kind. It does not envy, it does not boast, it is not proud. It does not dishonor others, it is not self-seeking, it is not easily angered, it keeps no record of wrongs. Love does not delight in evil but rejoices with the truth. It always protects, always trusts, always hopes, always perseveres. Love never fails."

1 Corinthians 13:4-8a

I love checklists. There's something so gratifying about checking off each item.

This well-known passage from Corinthians is one of the most wonderful checklists. It can apply to many different kinds of relationships—those with our family members, romantic partners, and even our friends. Take a minute and consider your closest friends. Check off all the items that describe them.

My closest friends:

- ☐ Are patient and kind with me and others.
- ☐ Don't act envious or jealous.
- ☐ Are not boastful or arrogant.
- ☐ Respect me and take my feelings into consideration.
- ☐ Don't keep a list of everything I do wrong.
- ☐ Love truth and doing the right thing.
- ☐ Protect me and trust me.
- ☐ Continue to be my friends no matter what.

REFLECT

How'd your friends do? Were you able to check off a lot of those items? If so, you're blessed with some amazing friends. If you didn't check off many boxes, that's okay, too—make room in your life for God to lead you to faithful friends.

OBEY YOUR PARENTS

"Children, obey your parents in the LORD, for this is right. 'Honor your father and mother'—which is the first commandment with a promise—'so that it may go well with you and that you may enjoy long life on the earth.'"
Ephesians 6:1-3

If you've been going to church for any length of time, you've likely heard sermons or Sunday school lessons about obeying your parents. Your youth pastor has probably talked about it, too.

The Bible teaches us that obeying and honoring your mom and dad is the right thing to do. And it promises a rich reward if you do: a long, well-lived life.

What does obeying your parents look like in a practical sense? Here's an example: When I was 16, I was dating the cutest guy at my school. He played basketball and drove a Jeep, and I was crazy about him. But my dad had some concerns about him. Dad was convinced that something wasn't right, and he asked me to break up with him.

It was so hard, but I trusted my earthly father, believing he had deeper insight into the situation. And it turned out that my dad's advice was solid. My boyfriend struggled with drug problems and drinking heavily—both of which he'd kept a secret from me. Not long after we broke up, he entered rehab and began to get some help.

As unpleasant as the breakup was at the time, I can look back and tell you that I'm glad I listened to my dad. Obeying parents isn't always easy, but there is protection and promise when we do.

REFLECT

Do you have an easy time or a hard time obeying your parents? What's one small way you can resolve to obey them this week?

ONE BODY, MANY PARTS

"For just as each of us has one body with many members, and these members do not all have the same function, so in Christ we, though many, form one body, and each member belongs to all the others. We have different gifts, according to the grace given to each of us."

Romans 12:4-6a

Have you ever been a part of a praise team, choir, or band? Everyone has his or her role to play. You've got to have instrumentalists: the drummer, guitar player, bass player, keyboard player, and maybe a few others. Typically, different voices sing different parts that combine to create one beautiful harmony.

Similarly, in the body of Christ, you are one of many members. The members all have specific roles to play. Some speak and teach, others counsel and give wisdom. There are some in the body who offer compassion and encouragement. Still others serve, show mercy, and organize—by working in the nursery or leading fundraisers for youth camp and people in need. Together, the members form one body—the church of Jesus Christ.

What part do you play? Do you have the heart of a teacher? Or perhaps you enjoy speaking to groups. Maybe you love to sing and lead in worship. Or maybe you're great at organizing and leading groups. Are you that person who listens well and offers wise counsel? Or the one who loves to serve the needs of others?

Whatever the case, your role is vital. Your gifts can edify other believers and build up the body of Christ. You are essential and needed.

REFLECT

What are two or three ways God has uniquely gifted you? What roles do you play at home, in your youth group, at church, or in the community? How else would you like to contribute?

FORGIVENESS, ALWAYS

"If we confess our sins, he is faithful and just and will forgive us our sins and purify us from all unrighteousness."
1 John 1:9

My friend Lauren called me in tears late on a Tuesday night as I was preparing for school the next day. She was crazy about her boyfriend, and in all of the emotion and excitement, she'd stayed out too late with him and they'd gone too far. She'd done things she couldn't take back, and she was consumed with regret and guilt. Can I share with you what I shared with Lauren? It's pretty simple—we serve a loving God who always forgives. If we take our sin and shame to him, he will forgive us, cleanse us, and wash away the stain, the dirt, the pain, and the shame.

Yes, there will be consequences to your sin. Terrible things can happen. If you lie, you will likely get caught. If you cheat on a test, you may fail a class or get suspended. Eating too much will make you sick. Taking drugs or drinking will impact your brain cells, your body, and your decision-making.

However, God's grace is enough to cover all of your sin, heal your shame, and restore your joy. All you need to do is confess your sins to him.

REFLECT

What's the worst thing you've ever done? Have you confessed it to the Lord? There's nothing too grave or horrible for him to forgive. Nothing!

THE GOLDEN RULE

"Do to others as you would have them do to you."
Luke 6:31

It seems like there are rules everywhere we look: on the road, in the classroom, at home, on the team, or in the band.

Rules protect us, inform us, and give us guidelines. Without stoplights, there would be more car accidents. Without rules in school, it would be hard to hear or learn. If there were no rules at home, there might be chaos. And the team or band rules are provided to help the whole group succeed.

The Bible provides many principles, guidelines, and rules. One of the most famous is the Golden Rule. It's actually quite straightforward: Treat others like you want to be treated. Do to others what you'd like them to do to you. Speak to your friends the way you'd like them to speak to you. Talk to your parents and teachers the way you'd like them to talk to you.

Does this work? Most of the time, yes. If you smile at someone in the hall at school, they'll likely smile back. If you are kind to a customer at work, they will probably be kind in return. Occasionally, you'll encounter someone who doesn't respond well. But you can't control that. Your job is to treat others the way that you want to be treated.

REFLECT

Have you practiced the Golden Rule? How have you seen it work? Plan to put it into practice at least once today.

DO NOT BE AFRAID

"The LORD is my light and my salvation—whom shall I fear? The LORD is the stronghold of my life—of whom shall I be afraid?"

Psalm 27:1

It's not just Halloween: People spend money throughout the year to be scared.

It sounds odd, but think about it. We spend huge amounts of money to ride scary rides at theme parks. People fork out hundreds of dollars to bungee jump, hang glide, skydive, zip line, and try other adventurous things. We pay to feel the adrenaline rush. But not everything daring in our lives has to do with entertainment.

The Bible gives words that can fill you with courage no matter what adventure you're on. Because the Lord is your light and your salvation, you don't have to fear anyone. The Lord is your stronghold.

Your fear today may not be a roller coaster. Instead, it may be an English test, a difficult friend, a sick family member, or a broken heart. Wherever you walk today, remember that God is right beside you as your light and your strength. You can do it.

REFLECT

What are you facing right now that will require God's light and strength in your life? Think of one step you can take to conquer your fear, and ask God to help you carry it out.

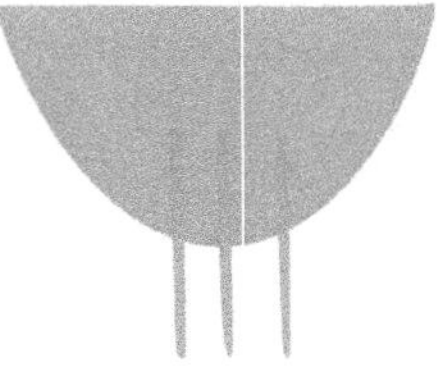

GOD LOVES EVERY FRECKLE

"Indeed, the very hairs of your head are all numbered. Don't be afraid; you are worth more than many sparrows."
Luke 12:7

It's an awesome thing to think about: God knows exactly how many hairs are on your head at this very minute. God knows what color your eyes are and how they change based on the colors you wear. He knows which of your teeth are crooked or have cavities. He's aware of every freckle on your skin and the sound of your laughter from afar.

Would it surprise you to know that he also keeps up with everything you think? Before you speak a word, he knows what you're going to say. Your deepest hurts and biggest dreams: He's familiar with them, too. His attention to the details of your life is unparalleled. Father God knows you better and more intimately than any person ever will.

If he can keep up with the little sparrows and other birds, he can keep up with you. So there's no reason to fear. Take every concern of your heart to the Lord in prayer. Talk over any issue with him. He loves you and deeply cares about your life.

REFLECT

God counts the hairs on your head—think about that for a minute. He's intimately interested in your life. Does that make you more inclined to talk to him? Follow that inclination.

THE SWEETNESS OF CONFESSION

"For as high as the heavens are above the earth, so great is his love for those who fear him; as far as the east is from the west, so far has he removed our transgressions from us."
Psalm 103:11-12

I worked at a summer camp during college, and my least favorite responsibility was cleaning out the camp pool, which was part of a natural body of water. All of the counselors got in fully dressed and walked through the muddy water, pulling out roots, weeds, and leaves. It was the grossest thing I've ever done. I don't think I've even been as muddy, sweaty, and stinky as I was that day. And I don't think a hot shower has ever felt better than the one I took afterward.

Confession is a lot like taking a hot shower when you are covered in mud, sweat, and dirt. To have the steaming hot water of grace flow over your mistakes, your sin, and your shame is overwhelming. To admit our sin to God, have him remove it, and come away forgiven is life altering.

The Bible tells us that God, in his great love, removes our sin so that it's as far from us as the east is from the west. God takes our sin and flings it away—never to be brought back upon us again.

REFLECT

When you confess to God and ask for forgiveness, he removes your sin forever. Is there anything you need to confess to God today?

STAND UNITED

"I appeal to you, brothers and sisters, in the name of our Lord Jesus Christ, that all of you agree with one another in what you say and that there be no divisions among you, but that you be perfectly united in mind and thought."

1 Corinthians 1:10

There is nothing quite like being part of a team. My varsity basketball team was one of the best in the city during my senior year. When my teammates and I all played together, we'd usually win the game. However, when we felt disjointed or out of sorts with each other, we'd struggle.

In our final game of our final season, we got very frustrated. As the opposing team scored more and more points, we started to pass the ball less, trying to win the game as individuals. Quarreling, blaming, and discord all added to that horrible loss. If we had been able to come together as a team, I think we could have won. But our lack of unity defeated us.

In this verse, God implores us to be brothers and sisters in Christ who work together. Sadly, divisions in churches, homes, and friendships not only hurt us but also hurt the body of Christ. Conversely, to be unified in purpose is to honor the wishes of our Savior and build greater community.

REFLECT

How unified are things in your home? At school? In your closest friendship? How can you personally bring more unity to each of these groups?

ALL THAT'S HIDDEN

"There is nothing concealed that will not be disclosed, or hidden that will not be made known. What you have said in the dark will be heard in the daylight, and what you have whispered in the ear in the inner rooms will be proclaimed from the roofs."

Luke 12:2-3

Secrets are those things we do in hiding, choices we make that no one else knows about. We tuck them away somewhere safe, hoping no one will ever find out. But the Bible reminds us that nothing will remain hidden forever. One day, everything will come to light.

God knows and sees everything. It's hard to comprehend, but he's able to perceive every action, thought, and reaction that takes place on this planet. He always has seen and he will continue to see. Nothing is hidden from him.

Despite this, we continue to hide our secrets from others, covering up our mistakes and missteps. That's been the human tendency since the Garden of Eden. When Adam and Eve ate the fruit that God told them not to eat, they tried to hide in their shame. People have been trying to hide ever since.

Instead of hiding your mistakes, what might happen if you admitted them to God? I believe some incredible healing will take place if you uncover all of your secrets and give them completely to our heavenly Father. What we uncover, he is able to cover, heal, and restore.

REFLECT

What's your biggest secret? What might happen if you talked it over with the Lord today? Would it also help if you shared your secret with a trusted friend?

SEE MORE CLEARLY

"Therefore, I urge you, brothers and sisters, in view of God's mercy, to offer your bodies as a living sacrifice, holy and pleasing to God—this is your true and proper worship. Do not conform to the pattern of this world, but be transformed by the renewing of your mind. Then you will be able to test and approve what God's will is—his good, pleasing, and perfect will."

Romans 12:1-2

One winter, my family and I were driving through the mountains in a dense fog. We could see only a few feet in front of our car. We were worried for our safety—unable to see the edge of the road or the cars around us. Then, as if someone blew the fog away, everything was suddenly clear. We could see ahead for miles and the stars were shining brightly in the sky.

Seeing clearly is critical, both while driving and in life.

To see clearly is to have greater vision, to be aware of obstacles, to be able to look down the road with confidence, and enjoy the stars in the sky. Would you like to see more clearly in your life? In God's system, better sight comes in the most unusual way: through surrender. As this text teaches, surrender means offering ourselves to God and being transformed by him.

This surrender and transformation leads to the most wonderful ability to see clearly, with an understanding of God's will for your life—an understanding that comes from yielding yourself to him completely.

To yield is to put your "yes" on the table and follow him.

REFLECT

Would you like to see more clearly? What are two or three ways God is asking you to say "yes" to him, at home, at school, or in your relationships?

WHO ARE YOUR PEOPLE?

"And let us consider how we may spur one another on toward love and good deeds, not giving up meeting together, as some are in the habit of doing, but encouraging one another—and all the more as you see the Day approaching."
Hebrews 10:24-25

Do you have some people who are your people? You know, a community of friends that you like to be with, around, and among?

I know a sports fan who visits his favorite arena at the University of Kentucky every time he travels there, even if he isn't going to see a game. Why? Because the Kentucky people are his people, and he loves to be with them, around them, and among them—especially on game day.

Scripture encourages us to get together with other believers—to have other Christian people with whom we spend time. Hanging out with these people spurs us on, inspires us, and gives us hope.

We can do this in connection with a local church. This type of community is also found in Bible studies, prayer groups, accountability groups, and friend groups.

REFLECT

Do you have some people who are your people? Do they spur you on to good deeds? If not, where might you find some believers who will inspire you and give you hope?

FIND CONTENTMENT

"Keep your lives free from the love of money and be content with what you have, because God has said, 'Never will I leave you; never will I forsake you.'"
Hebrews 13:5

Just for fun, let's do a little math. How many pairs of shoes do you own? What about purses? Is your closet filled with clothes? Are your dresser drawers stuffed? Do you have a home, a television, a cell phone, and a car to ride in or drive? Do you get to enjoy heat in the winter? Is there food to eat on a regular basis?

When you add up all these things, you will likely discover that you're very blessed. You have much to be thankful for. In fact, the average American is wealthy compared to people in many parts of the world.

But are you grateful and content with what you have? It's sometimes very difficult to not be sucked into the gravitational pull of accumulation: more money, more power, and more success. The magnets of greed are strong.

The Bible encourages us to be content with what we have—to enjoy what God has given us.

And there's great peace in that. You are always wealthy in God's company. He promises to never leave you or abandon you. He will always walk beside you, giving you the hope of his presence and his peace.

REFLECT

Does the lure of more money and success tug at your heart? If you're struggling with that, make a list of the possessions you already have that bring you joy. You might be surprised at how wealthy you already are.

GIVE GENEROUSLY

"Remember this: Whoever sows sparingly will also reap sparingly, and whoever sows generously will also reap generously. Each of you should give what you have decided in your heart to give, not reluctantly or under compulsion, for God loves a cheerful giver. And God is able to bless you abundantly, so that in all things at all times, having all that you need, you will abound in every good work."

2 Corinthians 9:6-8

My daughter is one of the most generous people I know. On every occasion, she knows exactly what to give, when to give it, and which people truly want to receive. Even as a little girl, she'd go to her room and wrap things she already owned, just to be able to give a gift.

She loved giving to those in need, and supporting missions projects at our church and children who were hospitalized. My girl wanted us to be involved. Being generous came naturally to her.

Generosity is a biblical trait. In these verses, we discover that God loves it when we give cheerfully and lavishly. We shouldn't give because we feel we should; giving from our hearts is more generous and authentic.

And God blesses our generosity. When you give to the needy, share with those less fortunate, and give your time or resources to help others, you can bet that God will return that goodness to you, giving you all you need.

Generous people thrive, flourishing and overflowing with God's blessings.

REFLECT

How has God blessed your generosity? How can you be more generous with your time, money, and gifts?

COMPREHENDING GOD'S LOVE

"And I pray that you, being rooted and established in love, may have power, together with all the LORD's holy people, to grasp how wide and long and high and deep is the love of Christ, and to know this love that surpasses knowledge—that you may be filled to the measure of all the fullness of God."

Ephesians 3:17-19

What's your favorite subject in school—the one that you love and master with ease? Why do you enjoy it? Is there a class you struggle with? Why do you think it's hard for you?

When I was a student, I loved anything in the language arts field—writing, reading, grammar, and social sciences. I avoided most math and science classes like the plague. Math, especially, was a subject I found difficult to comprehend. Everyone else seemed to be able to grasp algebra, but no matter how much I tried, I couldn't absorb it.

For many people, God's love is like algebra was for me—hard to comprehend. They might know about it, but they struggle to apply it to their lives.

In these verses, Paul prays that the people at Ephesus will be able to grasp how much God loves them. He wants them to know the width, height, and depth of God's love. Paul desired for them to be filled up with God's love to the fullest measure.

Do you realize how loved you are? Father God has incredible affection for you.

REFLECT

Take a moment and invite God to show you how much he loves you. Ask him to give you a greater comprehension of the depth, height, and width of this love.

SECURE IN YOURSELF

"Therefore I tell you, do not worry about your life, what you will eat or drink; or about your body, what you will wear. Is not life more than food, and the body more than clothes?"
Matthew 6:25

I know a girl who's an impressive public speaker. You'd never guess that she once struggled with insecurity and self-doubt. She will tell you that for many years she was quiet and withdrawn, careful not to say the wrong thing. She was too afraid of making a mistake. Underlying her insecurity was a drive to be perfect.

Maybe you can relate. Most people battle feelings of inadequacy and insecurity from time to time. For some, it's severe and debilitating. For others, feelings of self-doubt fluctuate depending on the situation.

There are so many things that can cause insecurity. Social media is just one culprit. You scroll through post after post showing people's fabulous vacations, decadent meals out, and impeccably styled selfies. It's easy to feel left out when everyone's lives look better than yours.

Insecurity can attack you in the real world, too, on those days when it seems like everyone at school has cuter outfits, gets more attention, or scores higher on tests than you do. When you feel this way, it's important to know that you're not alone. Everyone struggles, and young women are especially vulnerable—it's so easy to let insecurity ruin our day. Remember: Life is more than the food you eat and the clothes you wear.

To overcome feelings of self-doubt, train your mind to focus on this one fact: Father God created you masterfully and loves you unconditionally. To him, you are amazing!

REFLECT

When do you feel most insecure? What causes you to doubt yourself? When those feelings start to overcome you, write down at least three things you like about yourself.

KINDNESS IS ALWAYS IN STYLE

"Be kind and compassionate to one another, forgiving each other, just as in Christ God forgave you."
Ephesians 4:32

Styles and trends come and go. Just look at anyone who wore flared jeans, bold stripes, polyester fabrics, and those crazy stacked shoes in the 1970s.

Though fashion trends may change, kindness is always in style. Kindness, compassion, and forgiveness are timeless traits. They never get old or lose their appeal. Jesus himself displayed these traits, and we can strive for them, too.

How can you add more kindness to your style? Maybe you could be more patient with your brother or sister? Perhaps you could roll your eyes at your parents a little less often? When someone's struggling, you could listen to them. When your teammate scores a goal in practice, you could congratulate them. It doesn't take much to be kind—just a little extra effort and attention.

REFLECT

Is kindness part of your style? If so, how do you include it in your day? What's one way you might put on kindness today?

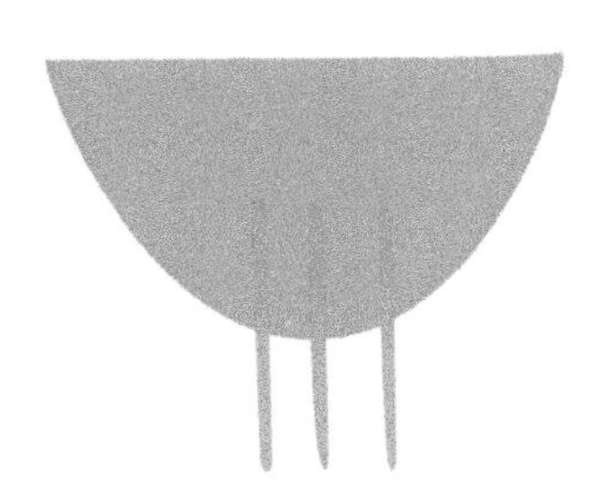

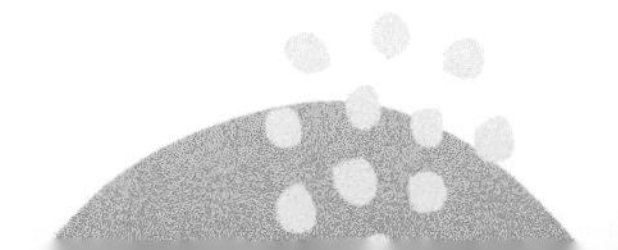

MIRACLES STILL HAPPEN

"I am the LORD, the God of all mankind. Is anything too hard for me?"
Jeremiah 32:27

It's one of the coolest things I've ever witnessed. My friend was very sick with cancer, and we began to pray for her healing. The church community prayed. Friends at school prayed. Neighbors prayed. Everyone was praying. When she went for her next screening, her doctors were amazed. The cancer was completely gone.

My friend's story is proof that miracles still happen and God still answers prayers. However, sometimes we stop believing that he can and will perform miracles—maybe because he doesn't always provide what we hoped for exactly how we imagined it. Or it could be that we haven't had the courage to ask him to do something amazing.

Whatever the case, the truth remains: Nothing is too difficult for God. So what do you need him to do in your life? What's one thing that would be a miracle to you? Why not pray about it? No request is too large or too small. If it matters to you, it matters to God.

Perhaps you've been longing to have a best friend to hang out with, laugh with, and talk to. Or maybe you'd love to have a date, an acceptance letter to college, or an opportunity to sing. Ask God for these things. He can easily handle them all.

REFLECT

Take a minute to write down a few things you'd love for God to do in your life. Then pray about these things until God answers. Have faith in his ability.

PROTECT YOURSELF ONLINE

"Turn my eyes away from worthless things; preserve my life according to your word."
Psalm 119:37

It's hard to believe that the Internet has existed for decades now. Today, we can use it to do homework, build friendships, and communicate with people around the world. But there's scary stuff online, too. Cyberbullying, fake friends, hackers, security breaches, stolen identities, and cruel behavior, just to name a few. So how can you be more careful online? Here are a few tips that may help:

- Limit your time online—especially late at night.
- Set up strong passwords for all of your accounts, and update them regularly.
- Exercise extreme caution when talking to someone you don't know. You can never be sure if the person you're chatting with is who he claims to be. If he seems too cute, too nice, or too good to be true, it's because he probably is.

If you ever feel like you're being stalked, bullied, or harassed, let an adult or older friend know. It's never okay for someone to speak unkindly to you or about you online. This verse from the Psalms encourages us to turn our eyes from looking at worthless, empty, false, and vain things. It's so easy to get pulled into all sorts of drama online, but at the end of the day, it adds no value to your life.

REFLECT

Are you experiencing anything online that makes you uncomfortable or scared? If so, share what you're going through with a trusted adult or older friend. You may succeed in helping others as well as yourself.

ALL THINGS WORK TOGETHER FOR GOOD

"And we know that in all things God works for the good of those who love him, who have been called according to his purpose."
Romans 8:28

One of my seminary professors used the term "life grid" to describe the unique way that each person looks at his or her life. Think of it like wearing a pair of sunglasses all the time. It's the filter through which you view every person, situation, and event in your life. It's your frame of reference and your worldview. For the most part, your relationships and experiences shape your unique life grid.

Why does this matter? Because your life grid frames and impacts everything you think and believe about God. Through the lens of your life grid, you likely view God in one of three ways:

- As a sovereign—completely capable of handling your life and bringing its events together for your good and his glory.
- As distant and completely uninvolved in your life. You may think he's too busy taking care of the world to be bothered with you.
- Somewhere in the middle. He may be involved or he may not.

My prayer for you is that your life grid will always view God as sovereign. I pray you will trust him completely with everything. See him as capable, loving, kind, and involved in your life. Believe he can and will work all things together for good as you grow in your love for him.

REFLECT

So, what's your life grid view on God? Is he involved? Distant? Somewhere in between? How might you learn to trust him more?

YOU HAVE A BEAUTIFUL GIFT

"Flee from sexual immorality. All other sins a person commits are outside the body, but whoever sins sexually, sins against their own body."
1 Corinthians 6:18

There is something about Christmas, birthdays, and parties that makes me feel giddy. I absolutely love gift giving. In fact, I like the giving of gifts more than the receiving of gifts. To see someone open a present and light up with joy over what's inside is so gratifying.

What about you? Would you rather give a gift or receive one? Have you ever thought about the idea that giving yourself to another person sexually is like giving them a beautiful gift? If you allow someone to mess with your bow or pull back a little tape and look under a corner of the wrapping, you are giving them part of your purity gift—a part of your soul.

You only get to give the gift one time. Once you give the gift, it's unwrapped, opened, and used. The giving of the gift will never be the same again.

The Bible tells us to flee from sexual immorality. This means avoiding all forms of sex and sexual activity until you're married. At that time, you give the beautiful gift of yourself to only one person: your husband.

You get to choose to give yourself to someone else. Why not make a vow to the Lord to save your beautiful gift until marriage? I did, and I can promise you that it was well worth the wait.

REFLECT

Have any guys pressured you to engage in sexual activity? Have you ever felt tempted? To help stand your ground, ask a trusted friend to hold you accountable to your commitment to save sex for marriage. Talk to this friend weekly and give her permission to ask hard questions.

BE REFRESHING

"A generous person will prosper; whoever refreshes others will be refreshed."
Proverbs 11:25

When you think about the word "refreshing," what comes to mind? Maybe a tall glass of ice water or Gatorade? A hot shower after a sweaty workout? Hugs can be refreshing. Hot meals can be refreshing. Even a good night of sleep can be sweetly refreshing.

To refresh is to replenish, revitalize, restore, renew, and energize. And the word doesn't only describe physical health. We can also be refreshed spiritually, mentally, and emotionally.

So, what does this look like? A refreshing friend is one who makes you feel better after being in their presence. To be with a refreshing friend lifts you up, encourages you, and makes your life sweeter.

Are you a refreshing friend to others? When your friends spend time with you, do they leave encouraged and full of hope? Do you lift others up? The Bible promises that the person who offers refreshment will have it returned to them in kind.

REFLECT

Who is the most refreshing person you know? How do you feel after spending time with this person? How can you be a more generous and refreshing friend to those in your life?

RESISTING TEMPTATION

"When tempted, no one should say, 'God is tempting me.' For God cannot be tempted by evil, nor does he tempt anyone; but each person is tempted when they are dragged away by their own evil desire and enticed. Then, after desire has conceived, it gives birth to sin."
James 1:13-15

It can happen so quickly. One minute you are floating on a raft in the ocean, close to the beach. The next minute, you're far from where you started and worried about how to get back. As you float, the ocean's currents and the winds pull you away from where you started.

Drifting can happen on the water, and it can happen in your daily life. For instance, you can have the most amazing Sunday at church, read your devotional on Monday and Tuesday, and then miss a few days. By Friday, you've drifted away and found yourself in places you said you'd never go.

Temptation works much like the currents of the ocean. One minute, you are standing strong, living for Jesus with abandon. The next minute you are being slowly dragged away by a desire that pops up on your radar. It pulls at your heart and eventually sucks you into sin, which always leads to pain.

God doesn't tempt us. That's not his way. Instead, we get dragged away by our own evil desires. We must begin to be aware of the subtle pull of sin on our lives by spending time in the Bible, journaling regularly, praying often, and becoming connected with friends and peers who are trying to live for Christ.

REFLECT

Temptation feels like being on a raft in the ocean and drifting away from the shore. What can you do when you start feeling the pull to sin?

SEEK GOD'S COUNSEL

"If any of you lacks wisdom, you should ask God, who gives generously to all without finding fault, and it will be given to you."

James 1:5

When your life gets challenging and you need wisdom, whom do you call? Are there older, wiser friends in your life who give you great counsel? Perhaps you have a teacher or youth worker who listens to you and advises you on important matters. Or maybe you talk to an older sister, a cousin, or a parent when you're in a bind.

We all need insightful people to confide in, learn from, and talk to—especially when we're uncertain about a situation. I've sought the wise counsel of a friend many, many times. It's wonderful to have others to walk with us through the challenges of life.

In addition, the Bible encourages us to talk matters of the heart over with God. When you need wisdom, he promises to give it to you generously. All you have to do is ask him for it.

Do you need wisdom today? With a strained friendship? With a teacher? With your boyfriend? About your future? You can take anything you are dealing with to God and invite him to enlighten you. Ask him to give you eyes to see, ears to hear, and the mind to grasp what you need to do in this situation.

REFLECT

What is one way you need wisdom today? Is there a situation that challenges you? Reach out to a trusted friend and talk it over. Pray about it and ask God to give you wisdom.

BE A LIGHT

"You are the light of the world. A town built on a hill cannot be hidden. Neither do people light a lamp and put it under a bowl. Instead they put it on its stand, and it gives light to everyone in the house. In the same way, let your light shine before others, that they may see your good deeds and glorify your Father in heaven."

Matthew 5:14-16

It was an extremely clear night. The air was cool, and my kids wanted to go outside and see the stars. Bundled up in jackets, we all bounded up onto the trampoline to lie on our backs and look up at the night sky. It was astonishing. Thousands of tiny lights dotted the expanse. God showed off that night by painting the darkness with beautiful splashes of light.

Light against the darkness: that's what believers are supposed to be. God created us to be little splashes of light painted across the dark expanse of humankind. Jesus instructs us to let our lights shine before other people. As our lights shine, people witness our kindness, grace, and mercy, and, hopefully, they'll want to know what makes us different.

Are you a bright light in this world? Honestly, it doesn't take much light to make a difference. Have you ever been home when the power went out? When you use the flashlight on your phone or light just one candle, the whole room is illuminated. You might feel like you're just a small candle, but you can still illuminate the world with God's love.

REFLECT

What are some simple ways you can be a light in your friend group? Neighborhood? School? Church? How can you shine a little brighter today?

GREAT HABITS TO PURSUE

"Let us then approach God's throne of grace with confidence, so that we may receive mercy and find grace to help us in our time of need."
Hebrews 4:16

Time alone with the Creator of the universe is absolutely necessary in my world. There is something about opening my Bible, talking with the Lord, and being quiet in his presence that changes me. When I take time to be with God each morning—after my coffee and breakfast and right before I head out the door—I am filled with mercy, grace, and confidence to face the day.

What about you? Could you use more mercy, grace, and confidence? Are you taking time each morning before school to approach God's throne? Or maybe you spend time with him before you go to bed? Either way, it's an indispensable habit to have. You may call it a devotional, a quiet time, a throne of grace, or a Bible study. No matter what you call it, I've discovered that I need it.

Think of it like filling a water bottle before you go for a run. You're going to need fresh water as you exercise. Similarly, you need a fresh filling of mercy and grace before you go and face the day. Otherwise, you head out into the world dry and thirsty.

REFLECT

Are you in the habit of spending time with God every day? If not, what might you need to change to begin this habit? Let time with God encourage you.

INVITE GOD TO BLESS YOU

"Jabez cried out to the God of Israel, 'Oh, that you would bless me and enlarge my territory! Let your hand be with me, and keep me from harm so that I will be free from pain.' And God granted his request."
1 Chronicles 4:10

From the time I first read this prayer, I've been praying in this way almost daily. I believe you could pray this prayer as well and begin to see God do amazing things in your life.

First, ask God to bless you. Invite him to open up the windows of heaven and pour out his goodness, grace, kindness, and blessings on your life. Tell him you don't want to miss out on anything he has in store for you. Next, ask the Lord to enlarge your territory; in other words, to grow and expand the impact that you can make on this planet.

Then ask God to keep his hand on you—in protection and power. Finally, ask him to keep you from harm, pain, and evil.

God granted Jabez's request. He has granted mine as well. And I believe he will grant yours.

REFLECT

For the next week, pray this prayer daily. At the end of each day, notice how God has worked in your life.

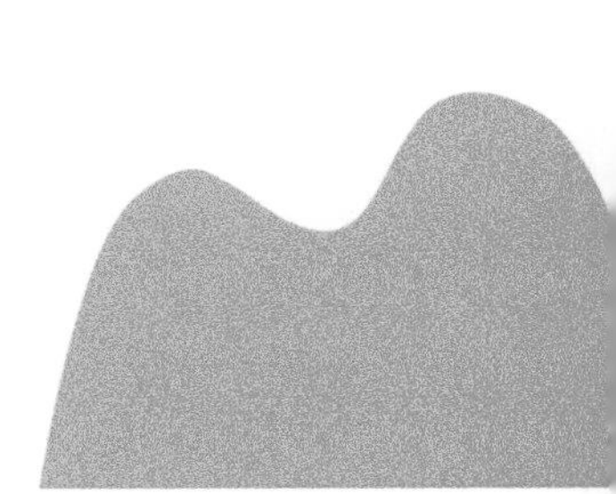

HEART FRIENDS

"After David had finished talking with Saul, Jonathan became one in spirit with David, and he loved him as himself."

1 Samuel 18:1

Name your five best friends. These are the people you love more than any others—the friends you most like to spend time with. Who did you choose and why?

In 1 Samuel, we read the story of David and Jonathan, two young warriors in the days when Saul was king. Scripture tells us that they became one in sprit and deeply loved each other as brothers. Other translations use words like "an immediate bond was formed between them"; they were "bound in friendship"; and "their hearts were knit together."

One of my friends likes to use the term "heart friends." These are the people whose hearts are knit together with yours. You understand each other deeply and connect on a soul level. Your spirits are bound together in unity and friendship. If you have at least one heart friend, you are truly blessed.

REFLECT

Go back to your list of best friends. Who are your heart friends—those with whom you are knit together? Heart friends stand by you, believe in you, and support you. Take a moment to thank God for these friendships, and do something today to show your heart friends how much you appreciate them.

GIVE THANKS

"Give thanks to the LORD, for he is good; his love endures forever."
Psalm 107:1

Gratitude is a popular word today. To be grateful is to be pleased, thankful, and appreciative. We express gratitude to our family, friends, teachers and coaches, youth ministers, our pastors and their wives, and to others who encourage us and support us.

The list of things I'm grateful for includes my gracious and supportive husband, laughing with my kids, hanging out with my funny dog, a wonderful home and neighborhood, the opportunity to write this devotional and speak to groups, my Bible study group, my friends, great food, and good health.

It's easy to turn that list into a prayer of thanks to God, the giver of all good gifts. Gratitude is always best when it's expressed. Don't keep it to yourself! Set it to music, journal about it, or share with friends the ways in which God has blessed you.

REFLECT

Take a moment and write down ten things you're grateful for today. What did you list? You might include family, friends, your home and school, and being able to eat delicious food. When you think about it, there are so many things to feel grateful for.

YOUR IDENTITY IN CHRIST

"But you are a chosen people, a royal priesthood, a holy nation, God's special possession, that you may declare the praises of him who called you out of darkness into his wonderful light."
1 Peter 2:9

My dog, Koda, is a fluffy, hyper Australian shepherd. We adopted him in March, and our life has never been the same. We're probably guilty of giving him too many toys, but his most important possession is a heart-shaped tag for his collar with his name engraved on it. We want people to know his name in case he gets separated from us.

Did you know that God has given you a tag to wear? You can't see it, but it hangs around your neck all the time. It says all of the names and identities that you have in Christ. The Bible tells us that God gives us name tags like "Chosen," "His Special Possession," "Daughter of the King," "Beloved," "Precious in His Sight," and so many more. One of my favorites is "Redeemed."

Just like our puppy is exceedingly precious to us, you are even more precious to Father God. He is crazy about you!

REFLECT

Of all the identities God has given you, which one do you love most?

JEALOUSY

"But if you harbor bitter envy and selfish ambition in your hearts, do not boast about it or deny the truth. Such 'wisdom' does not come down from heaven but is earthly, unspiritual, demonic."
James 3:14-15

Jealousy can grip us anytime: When you look at a friend's Instagram account and see she has more followers than you do. When your crush starts talking to another girl. When someone else gets the part or the highest grade.

Some people think women are more susceptible to jealousy than men. That's not surprising, given that the media is constantly sending us messages about what a "perfect" woman looks and acts like. As a result, when we see someone in real life who seems to conform to this ideal, we might feel envious of her.

I really struggle with jealousy, and I'll bet you do, too. We don't plan to be jealous or want to be jealous, but the feeling creeps in anyway. It's human nature.

Scripture discourages us from harboring selfish ambition, jealousy, and bitterness in our hearts. Instead, we have to recognize the truth about our jealousy and confess it to God. Then we lay down our jealousy and move forward.

When feelings of jealousy come over me, I've found that two things really help. First, I talk about my struggle with God and ask him to give me grace. Then I pray for the person I'm jealous of and ask God to bless them. Holding onto bitter feelings only amplifies the hurt you feel.

REFLECT

Is there anyone who you've been jealous of lately? Take a moment to pray for them and ask God's grace to come down upon them.

BE QUICK TO LISTEN

"My dear brothers and sisters, take note of this: Everyone should be quick to listen, slow to speak and slow to become angry."

James 1:19

A few weeks ago, I boarded a plane to head home from a trip. I was happily settled into my seat and catching up on some reading when a young man boarded the plane and plopped down right beside me. He was unshaven, wearing wrinkled clothes, and rather a mess. Honestly, I was tired and wanted to stay in my nice, safe bubble. But he said hello, and I replied. Then, for the duration of our two-hour flight, this young man shared his story with me.

I don't think I got in more than a few words—but I didn't truly mind. Apparently, he needed someone to listen to him. Sometimes people need to talk, and they really need someone to listen as they speak. I hope that when he arrived home, he felt better.

Listening is a lost art. We have two ears and one mouth, but most of us would rather speak than listen. In James, we are encouraged to be quick to listen, slow to speak, and slow to become angry. It's a real challenge!

There are people all around us who need us to be quick to listen. To give the gift of listening is to give the most incredible gift.

REFLECT

Is there a family member or friend who might need the gift of listening today? Can you commit to listening to their story, even if only for a few minutes?

GOD IS WITH YOU

"I will put my dwelling place among you, and I will not abhor you. I will walk among you and be your God, and you will be my people."
Leviticus 26:11-12

One of my favorite books of all time is a small paperback called *The Practice of the Presence of God*, written over 100 years ago by a lay brother who worked in the kitchen of a monastery. This little volume has been shared all over the world. Its main message is simple: God is always with you; try to enjoy his presence more.

The Bible tells us that God is with us. He walks among us and never leaves us. But do we really recognize and enjoy his presence? And how do we do that, exactly?

To enjoy God's presence is to intentionally become more aware of his nearness. Start your day with God. Tell him, "Good morning." Talk things over with him as you're getting dressed. As you're driving or walking to school, pray silently about the day ahead.

During the day, whether in the classroom or at home, take a few minutes and focus your attention on this thought: "God is with me right now." If someone hurts your feelings, quietly mention this to the Lord. Before you take a test, take a deep breath and lift up a prayer to God.

Enjoying God's presence isn't complicated, but it can be difficult. Life is busy and noisy, and it's easy to drown out the Lord. But we can experience his joy if we purposely look for him, talk to him, and continually remember that he walks right beside us.

REFLECT

How might you enjoy the Lord more? How can you include him in your day more regularly?

WHAT MATTERS MOST?

"But Martha was distracted by all the preparations that had to be made. She came to him and asked, 'LORD, don't you care that my sister has left me to do the work by myself? Tell her to help me!'
'Martha, Martha,' the LORD answered, 'you are worried and upset about many things, but few things are needed—or indeed only one. Mary has chosen what is better, and it will not be taken away from her.'"

Luke 10:40-42

This story about Mary and Martha reminds us of what matters most: time alone with Jesus. But, like Martha, we struggle to make time to sit at his feet. There's so much we need to get done. You likely have homework to do, papers to write, chores, piano practice, lacrosse practice, church events, and so many other obligations.

So how should you make more time for what matters most? How can you become more intentional about sitting at the feet of Jesus? For one thing, it helps to pick a time. Each day, at the same time, spend time with the Lord. It can be in the morning or afternoon, or at night.

Also, it helps to have a place to hang out with the Lord. Select a spot where you can be alone, quiet, and undistracted. Have all of your supplies in one place: a Bible, notebook, pen, and devotional. Keep them in that spot so you can easily find them each day.

Finally, time with Jesus is best if you have a plan. For example, you might plan to read a five-minute devotional, read one chapter in Proverbs, and then spend five minutes in prayer and journaling.

Time alone every day with Jesus makes everything in your life sweeter. It's definitely what matters most.

REFLECT

Do you spend daily time with Jesus? Do you have a time, a place, some materials, and a plan? If not, why not start today?

GROWING UP CHRISTIAN

"In fact, though by this time you ought to be teachers, you need someone to teach you the elementary truths of God's word all over again. You need milk, not solid food! Anyone who lives on milk, being still an infant, is not acquainted with the teaching about righteousness. But solid food is for the mature, who by constant use have trained themselves to distinguish good from evil."

Hebrews 5:12-14

Have you ever watched how quickly a little baby grows? Maybe you have a younger sibling, cousin, or friend whom you've watched grow up. Babies begin by only drinking milk. Then, at a few months old, they start eating solid foods like cereal or mashed-up veggies and fruits. Once they begin to eat solids, they grow rapidly.

When you first came to Christ, you were like a little infant. As a baby Christian, you drank in the simple teachings of the Bible. Others fed you spiritual food, and you enjoyed learning. However, if you want to continue to grow as a believer, you must take in more solid food—more substantial truth.

What does solid food do for you spiritually? It teaches you to distinguish between good and evil, to do what is right, and to know how to respond in every situation.

Where do you get more solid food for your spirit? You can grow from time spent reading and studying the Bible. You can grow deeper spiritually by hanging out with godly people, praying, getting involved in Bible study and worship, and by filling your mind with great Christian books, music, podcasts, and conversations.

REFLECT

Are you a spiritual baby—still drinking milk? Or are you growing as a Christian and taking in deeper truths? How can you mature in your faith?

GOD IS YOUR STRENGTH

"The LORD is my strength and my shield; my heart trusts in him, and he helps me. My heart leaps for joy, and with my song I praise him. The LORD is the strength of his people, a fortress of salvation for his anointed one."

Psalm 28:7-8

At my gym, there is a huge rack of dumbbells. The weights start at 5 pounds and go up to 100 pounds. On occasion, someone will grab weights of 40 to 50 pounds in each hand. I'm always amazed how easily these athletes can lift the weights over their heads without breaking much of a sweat.

Even more amazing is the strength of God in our lives. God is unbelievably strong. He lifts the weight of this world with ease. In fact, nothing is too difficult for him. Knowing this, your heart can safely trust in him. He can help you, strengthen you, and be a fortress of salvation for you.

How do you need God to be strong on your behalf today? Maybe you have a relationship, a test, or a crisis that needs to be infused with the power of Almighty God?

REFLECT

How do you need God to infuse power into your world right now? Take a few minutes to pray and give him every challenging situation you're facing. Lean on him and embrace his strength.

GIVE YOUR WORRIES TO GOD

"Look at the birds of the air; they do not sow or reap or store away in barns, and yet your heavenly Father feeds them. Are you not much more valuable than they? Can any one of you by worrying add a single hour to your life?"
Matthew 6:26-27

On any given day and in any given conversation, my friend Olivia can work herself up into a frenzy with worry. She worries about her appearance, her weight, her friends, her Instagram account, her boyfriend, what her friends are talking about, what someone said to her, her job, her classes, her family, how much money she has, and so much more. This sweet girl is a classic worrywart.

Know any worriers? Maybe you are one yourself? Worry is like a snowball rolling down a mountain. It starts small and grows massive by the time it reaches the bottom of the hill. It's a vicious cycle: Worry creates more worry, which leads to even more worry.

So how do you control it? The Bible tells us not to worry—at all. You weren't designed to be a worrier. It's not good for you and it doesn't accomplish anything. Worry is a total waste of time. Jesus reminds us that the birds in the air don't worry about anything because they know God will take care of them.

To win over worry, you must trust that your heavenly Father will take care of you. Either you trust in God's abilities, or you continue worrying. But you can't do both. What if you gave yourself permission not to worry? How might that feel?

REFLECT

On a piece of paper, write down five things that are worrying you right now. Then talk about them with God. Now, tear up the paper and throw it away—giving yourself permission not to worry about any of these things all day long.

FILL UP WITH POWER

"But he said to me, 'My grace is sufficient for you, for my power is made perfect in weakness.' Therefore I will boast all the more gladly about my weaknesses, so that Christ's power may rest on me. That is why, for Christ's sake, I delight in weaknesses, in insults, in hardships, in persecutions, in difficulties. For when I am weak, then I am strong."

2 Corinthians 12:9-10

I get migraines, and when they're bad, they're really bad. The pounding and pressure can be almost unbearable. And they can strike at the worst times—like one Christmas, when I was supposed to be the guest speaker at a dinner and all I could do was lie still in my bed, feeling awful.

I had exhausted all of my options to alleviate the pain. So I got out my phone and texted all of my friends. I explained the situation and asked them to pray for relief of my headache so I could speak.

As I drove to the event, my head was still throbbing. However, I knew God wanted me to press on. Amazingly, at the moment I drove into the church parking lot, the migraine eased up. I met with the women, spoke, and ministered, feeling great strength, power, and peace. In my weakness, God's power was perfected.

That's what his grace is able to do: give us all that we need, no matter how we feel or what's going on in our lives. When you're struggling in class; if your sister or brother is driving you crazy; if you don't feel good about yourself: In all of these situations and more, God can fill you with his power and grace. When you're weary, God's grace can give you strength.

God's grace is enough—more than enough—for you.

REFLECT

Next time you're feeling weak, pray to God and ask him to fill you up with his power. Surrender to his ability to fill you with grace and healing.

CHOOSE JOY

"Though the fig tree does not bud and there are no grapes on the vines, though the olive crop fails and the fields produce no food, though there are no sheep in the pen and no cattle in the stalls, yet I will rejoice in the LORD, I will be joyful in God my Savior."

Habakkuk 3:17-18

I remember one of my most disappointing moments in high school. One of the guys on the football team had been talking to me in class. I thought he was so cute. It seemed we were really connecting—until another girl began to flirt with him. Eventually, he chose the other girl over me. My heart was crushed.

In Habakkuk, the prophet is lamenting all of the things that are going wrong in his life. And yet, he says he will be joyful in God his Savior. Habakkuk chooses joy even when his life isn't perfect.

You can do the same. You might find yourself going solo to the homecoming dance or the prom. You might look in the mirror and wish you were taller or thinner. Maybe you feel lonely, left out, disappointed, or frustrated. No matter what's threatening to steal your joy, you can still hold onto hope.

How? By choosing to rejoice in God your Savior and to enjoy your relationship with him. To do this, you need to spend time with him. Get a good Bible that you can easily read and understand. Begin to talk to God like you talk to your friends. Find a good church or Bible study you can attend. The joy of the Lord is your strength. Choose to be joyful in life, and you will find your struggles fade away in time.

REFLECT

Has anything happened this week that stole your joy? Refocus your attention on the joy of the Lord.

EXERCISE SELF-CONTROL

"But the fruit of the Spirit is love, joy, peace, forbearance, kindness, goodness, faithfulness, gentleness and self-control. Against such things there is no law."
Galatians 5:22-23

My son is an amazing young adult who has surrendered his life to the Lord. To continue to stay close to God, he and a few other young men formed an accountability group. It includes a program and app called Covenant Eyes that monitors what they look at online. It keeps them accountable to each other, encourages self-control, and helps them stay on the path of what is right and pure.

Wouldn't it be great if there were similar programs that monitored our thoughts and what we say? We could call them "Covenant Thoughts" and "Covenant Mouths." We'd get an alert every time our minds began to worry or our mouths started to say something unkind.

Since those programs don't exist, we lean on Scripture. The Bible tells us that we grow in self-control by staying close to the Lord. As we stay close, his Spirit fills us with the gifts of love, joy, peace, gentleness, and self-control. These gifts are available on a daily basis, but in order to receive them, we must be sensitive to the Spirit.

For example, when your little brother makes you angry, the Spirit will offer you a slice of self-control. You can choose to take the fruit or react harshly. When a friend speaks to you sarcastically, the Spirit offers you the chance to respond with love.

REFLECT

When is it most difficult for you to maintain self-control? Is there someone who really pushes your buttons and upsets you? Allow the Spirit to help you with this person.

FILLED WITH PEACE

"Peace I leave with you; my peace I give you. I do not give to you as the world gives. Do not let your hearts be troubled and do not be afraid."
John 14:27

A life filled with peace allows us composure and faith even in hard times. It's like floating in saltwater: the waves come, but your natural buoyancy keeps you on the surface, the ocean constantly lifting you back up. Peace powers the life of a believer. Without peace, you might feel as though you're struggling to tread water, constantly fighting in all areas of your life. Peace is a deep sense of calm that you can have in the depths of your soul. It's a tranquility, a quietness, and a composure that lifts you up even during the hardest moments in life. When filled with God's peace, you can take on the waves of life and know that you will rise to the surface on the other side.

Jesus promised peace to his disciples, and he promises his peace to you. You can enjoy this gift of God's Spirit that will flood your heart and enable you not to be troubled or afraid.

REFLECT

How has God's peace helped and empowered you? If you haven't experienced it, pray and ask him to fill you up with his peace.

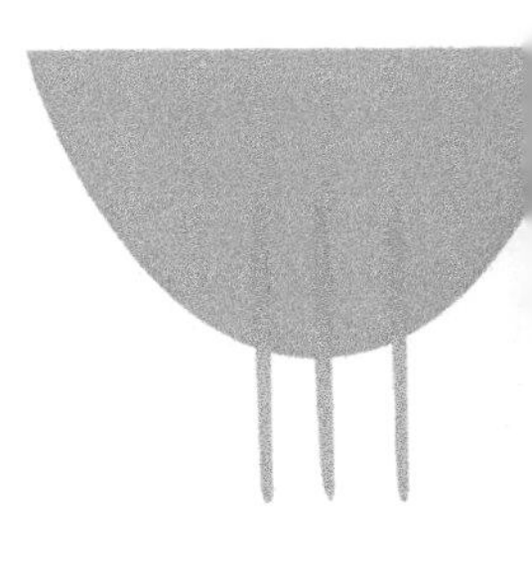

THE ARMOR OF GOD

"Therefore put on the full armor of God, so that when the day of evil comes, you may be able to stand your ground, and after you have done everything, to stand. Stand firm then, with the belt of truth buckled around your waist, with the breastplate of righteousness in place."

Ephesians 6:13-14

Each week, my Bible study teacher would mention this verse. If she said it once, she said it a hundred times. In particular, she'd highlight the phrase "After you have done everything to stand. Stand."

When you put on the full armor of God, you'll be able to stand your ground. This verse tells us that the armor of God includes truth, righteousness, and peace. In addition, arm yourself with faith, the Bible, and the power of your salvation so you are ready to stand firm.

As a teen, whom or what must you stand firm against? The list is endless. Yours may include teachers and professors whose beliefs challenge yours, cruel kids in school, the media, and challenges at home. You have to stand against bullies, lies, gossip, discouragement, and loneliness.

Standing is not easy, but it's part of the Christian life. Refusing to see a movie or read a novel with explicit scenes. Leaving a party when things get uncomfortable or out of hand. Refusing to drink, cuss, or experiment with drugs. Standing might mean that sometimes, you'll stand alone. When that happens, grab your armor, suit up, and keep standing.

REFLECT

What makes you want to sit down or sit out? Are you struggling to stand today? How can you fight on?

THE POWER OF MUSIC

"LORD, you are my God; I will exalt you and praise your name, for in perfect faithfulness you have done wonderful things, things planned long ago."
Isaiah 25:1

What songs are on your favorite playlist? Do you listen to any worship music? The music you listen to impacts your thinking, your attitude, and even your mood. That's why praise music is a wonderful tool for drawing closer to God. When you listen to it, it directs your attention toward heaven.

When you allow praise music to flow through your car speakers or earbuds, something happens deep within your spirit that lifts your focus toward God. Worship music ushers you into the Lord's presence—directly into his throne room. As we lift up our Savior, our spirits are lifted.

Every Wednesday night, I practice with our church choir, singing and praising with our voices. On my way home, I always feel so refreshed. Spending time exalting God and all he's done boosts my spirits and allows me to sense God's presence in a real and meaningful way.

REFLECT

What are you listening to? Does your favorite music lift your spirits? Ask friends, family, or members of your church community to recommend inspirational songs for you to add to your playlist.

DEALING WITH BULLIES

"Be strong and courageous. Do not be afraid or terrified because of them, for the LORD your God goes with you; he will never leave you nor forsake you."
Deuteronomy 31:6

Bullies come in all shapes and sizes. If you've been bullied, you understand the challenge. During my freshman year of college, I had a suitemate who was smart and funny. She was liked by some, but a bully to many. With her quick wit and sharp tongue, she could cut you to shreds without even batting an eye. No one wanted to upset her or get in her crosshairs for fear that she would make life miserable.

What can you do if someone is bullying you or a friend? First, you can pray about the situation. Hold onto a Scripture verse that gives you confidence. Be strong and courageous knowing that God goes with you and will never leave you. You should also talk to a trusted adult. Let a teacher, coach, or parent know about what's going on, and ask them to carefully handle this situation.

Dealing with my suitemate helped me learn that picking on those around her made her feel stronger. The bullying wasn't really about the people she bullied—it was her way of coping with her own weakness. In the end, she was a challenge, but a brief one. I didn't spend much time with her, choosing instead to make friends who respected and cared for me.

Bullying is a serious matter, but it doesn't have to ruin you. It can make you a stronger, more compassionate person. I am a much kinder person today because of what I experienced.

REFLECT

Have you had to deal with bullying, or had a friend or sibling who's been bullied? How did you respond? What did you learn from the situation?

TRANSITIONING TO ADULTHOOD

"When I was a child, I talked like a child, I thought like a child, I reasoned like a child. When I became a man, I put the ways of childhood behind me."
1 Corinthians 13:11

When my daughter was in sixth grade, she invited a few friends over to play after school one day. Her bedroom door was locked, and it was very quiet. I began to wonder what they were doing.

I tapped on the door and asked if everything was okay. Voices from inside the room assured me that everything was fine, so I left them alone. But, after another hour had passed, I was dying to know what was going on.

So I knocked again. My daughter opened the door, and I saw dolls and doll clothes spread out all over her room. My daughter and her friends were playing dolls, and they didn't want anyone to know. They felt self-conscious about playing with their childhood toys.

Letting go of childhood can be difficult. Growing from childhood to adulthood is a process—sometimes a long one. You likely fluctuate between feeling like a girl and feeling like a woman. It's a normal part of growing up.

However, as you grow, you should start feeling, sounding, and acting more like a woman than a young girl. You'll begin to put certain habits behind you—for instance, petty envy, impatience, and the tendency to act out your feelings all the time. When you let go of the habits that no longer serve you, you'll find a new confidence and peace.

REFLECT

Growing up can be challenging. Talk to your mom, aunt, or another trusted adult about how they navigated the transition from childhood to adulthood.

THE STORY OF YOUR LIFE

". . . being confident of this, that he who began a good work in you will carry it on to completion until the day of Christ Jesus."
Philippians 1:6

To me, there's nothing better than a compelling story that draws me in from the very first page and keeps me hooked all the way through to the end. Sometimes I cheat and read the last page before I'm done. Then I keep reading, eager to see how the events of the story fall into place.

This verse reminds us that God has already read the story of your life. He was there at the beginning. He's here with you in the middle, every day. And he knows how the story is going to end. Hills and valleys, painful and exhilarating, bitter and sweet: The Lord has seen all of your days—past, present, and future.

Scripture tells us that the God who began the work in your life will carry it out to completion until the day you meet him in glory. He will finish what he started in your life. It's ultimately his responsibility to make you into the amazing woman he designed you to be.

This means you can trust God with your present and your future. If you're feeling nervous or uncertain about a transition you have to make, trust in him. As you prepare to enter high school; if you have to move to a new city or state; if you're filling out college applications: No matter what's happening in your life, you can put your faith in God's perfect plans for your future.

REFLECT

Are you going through a transition that's making you feel uncertain about the future? Ask God to give you the faith to see him working out his plans in your life.

SEEING INTO THE FUTURE

"'For I know the plans I have for you,' declares the LORD, 'plans to prosper you and not to harm you, plans to give you hope and a future.'"
Jeremiah 29:11

In school, we would play with pieces of paper folded into origami fortune-tellers. Someone would write out all sorts of answers on the page before folding it. You'd ask a question, choose a number, and then your friend would manipulate the fortune-teller until it gave an answer.

Everyone lined up to play this game. In fact, people fought over having a turn. Why? Because everyone wants to know what the future looks like.

In this Scripture, God tells us exactly what he's planning for our lives: He will prosper us and give us a wonderful future. You can rest secure in the knowledge that God has amazing plans ahead for your life. As you are going into your next class, your next project, your next test, or something else entirely, you can be certain that God is at work in your life.

Maybe you don't sense him or see him, but he's there, working closely behind the scenes and making sure things go as they should.

REFLECT

How have you seen God work in your life? How have you sensed his hand on you? What excites you most about your future?

RAISE YOUR VOICE

"For the Spirit God gave us does not make us timid, but gives us power, love and self-discipline."
2 Timothy 1:7

What art or creative expression do you most enjoy? Maybe you like to sing? Or play an instrument? Or dance? Possibly you're a painter, a sculptor, or a photographer. Maybe—like me—you love social media, blogging, and writing. Or maybe you love to teach, lead, organize, or make people laugh.

Whatever your creative expression, I encourage you to do it with courage. Do it with all of your might. Raise your voice and be who God created you to be. The Bible tells us that his Holy Spirit doesn't make us timid; rather, it gives us power, love, and self-discipline.

God created you to shine, to stand tall, and to be bold. So be you—and don't hold back.

REFLECT

What do you feel like God has created you to do? Are you raising your voice and being bold in your pursuits? If not, what's holding you back?

MAKE A DIFFERENCE

"Now may the God of peace, who through the blood of the eternal covenant brought back from the dead our LORD Jesus, that great Shepherd of the sheep, equip you with everything good for doing his will, and may he work in us what is pleasing to him, through Jesus Christ, to whom be glory for ever and ever. Amen."

Hebrews 13:20-21

Agnes Gonxha Bojaxhiu was a nun and missionary who devoted her life to caring for the sick and the poor. Standing only five feet tall, she touched the lives of countless people through her work and the organizations she started. Although she was trained to be a teacher and a school principal, her life changed during a train ride to Darjeeling, India. It was at this time that she sensed God calling her to the slums to care for those who had nothing.

We know her as Mother Teresa. She was a woman whose life made a huge difference.

Would you like to make a difference in this world? How might God use you to make a dent in the world's problems? It could be through something you invent or create. You may change the world with your voice or your talent. Father God can use your willingness, your obedience, and your surrendered life to make an incredible difference in your school, church, neighborhood, and community.

REFLECT

What can you do to make a difference in your community? How would you like God to use you?

FOCUS ON TODAY

"Do not boast about tomorrow, for you do not know what a day may bring."
Proverbs 27:1

None of us have any idea what tomorrow may bring—or next week or month, for that matter. To face the future, we really have just one option: We must make the most of today.

How can we do this? First, love God with all of your heart. Living in a close, loving relationship with Jesus fills your life with hope and purpose. Second, love other people well. Enjoying the people God places in your life will give you joy and meaning.

Get up every morning and ask God what he wants you to do that day. Pray and invite him to make you sensitive to the promptings of his Spirit. As you walk through today, listen for his voice and watch for his hand at work around you.

Surrendered to him, you will get to enjoy his gifts and blessings and make the most of your time.

REFLECT

How can you make the most of today? Ask God to help you listen to the promptings of his Spirit.

INDEX OF TOPICS

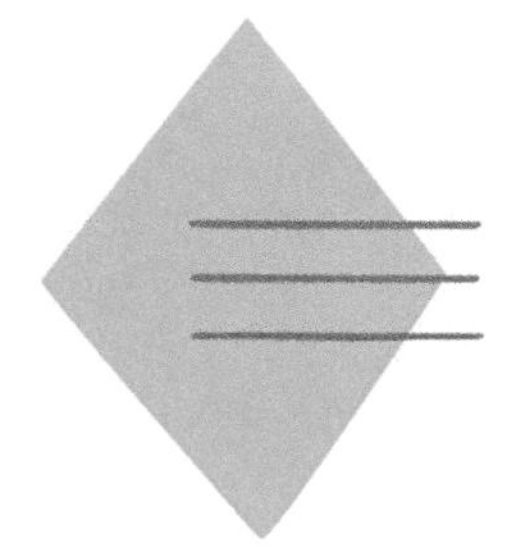

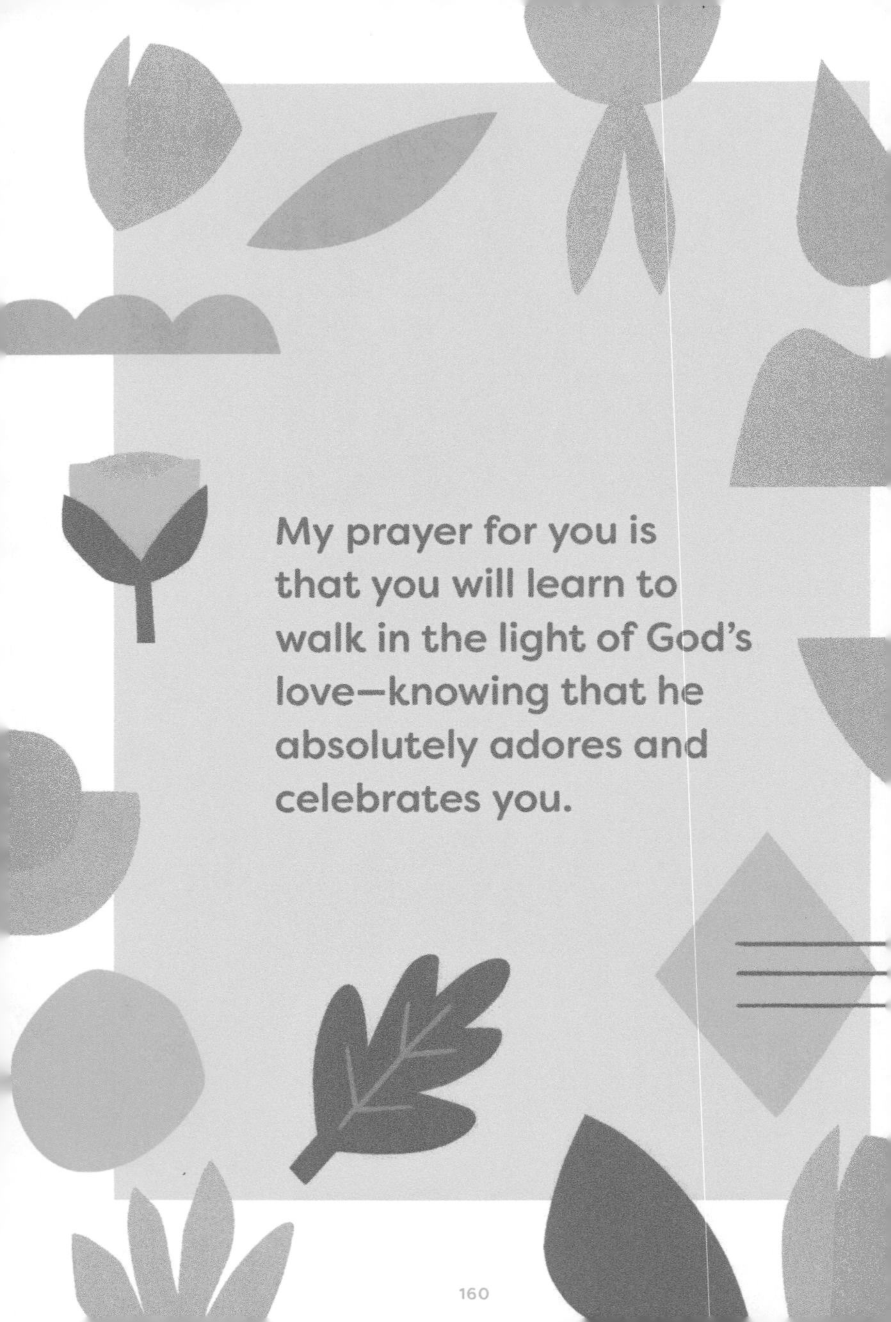

My prayer for you is that you will learn to walk in the light of God's love—knowing that he absolutely adores and celebrates you.

ACKNOWLEDGMENTS

Every major writing project requires a team of people to move it from an idea on a page to an actual published book. I'm so blessed by the wonderful people who helped make this dream a reality.

Thank you to my family for your support, your prayers, and your patience as I completed this project. I also really appreciate our brainstorming and idea sessions. You guys are the best!

Additionally, I'm grateful for my friends and fellow bloggers who have cheered me on throughout this endeavor. Thank you for believing in me and spurring me onward to greater things.

Big hugs to my launch team and all of those who assisted in spreading the word about this devotional. Thank you for sharing, posting, pinning, and announcing this book with such joy and enthusiasm.

Finally, I'd like to thank the amazing team at Callisto Media. Special thanks to Bridget Fitzgerald and Erin Klabunde for your time and your wise suggestions. You have been a huge help!

ABOUT THE AUTHOR

MELANIE REDD is a speaker, author, and teacher with a Master's in Christian Education. She loves to encourage, equip, train, and motivate other women. She wrote Sunday school curriculum and magazine articles for LifeWay Resources before launching her own ministry. You'll find Melanie encouraging a friend at a local coffee shop, cheering on a group of MOPS, writing an article for her blog, working on her latest book, and spending time in prayer with friends—when she's not traveling to speak at colleges, retreats, conferences, and church events. She's an energetic woman who loves to share the love of Christ with everyone around her.

Above all, Melanie is a pastor's wife and a mom who loves spending time with her family in the suburbs outside of Memphis, Tennessee.

CPSIA information can be obtained
at www.ICGtesting.com
Printed in the USA
BVHW050709050520
578821BV00003B/3

9 781641 523370